PERFORMANCE POWER

Transforming Stress Into Creative Energy

Dr. Irmtraud Tarr Krüger

English translation by
Dr. Edward H. Tarr

PERFORMANCE POWER

TRANSFORMING STRESS INTO CREATIVE ENERGY

© Summit Books
P. O. Box 26850
Tempe, Arizona 85285-6850

© by Dieter Breitsohl AG
Literarische Agentur Zürich 1993

© English edition:
Summit Books,
a division of Summit Records, Inc.

Executive Producers: Thomas Bacon,
Ralph Sauer, J. Samuel Pilafian, Dietrich Sauer

Project Supervisor: David R. Hickman

Cover Design: Tim Fisher

Photographs: Bob Carey Studios, Phoenix, Arizona

Layout: Cheryl Gorder

ISBN 1-887210-00-8

CONTENTS ━━━━━

PART TWO: PERFORMANCE POWER

Performance Power

To my mother,
from whom I learned
not to be afraid

Preface

This book is about a phenomenon well known to most of us: performance anxiety (or its synonym, stage fright). What public speaker has never experienced weak knees and sweaty palms, what runner or swimmer the "butterflies in the belly", what teacher the vision of being eaten alive by the "dear little ones" he faces, what trumpeter the terrors of the high C, what soccer goalie the specific fears of the eleven-meter goal attempt, the field-goal kicker the infinite possibilities of failure? If we care to admit it, probably all of us are intimately familiar with this specific fear. It is conjured up by being in the limelight or onstage, subject to the censure of our referees and rivals.

True performance power comes to only a few of us. The rest of us are impaired by our anxiety. If we want to attain the power which could rightfully be ours, we will therefore have to find out first what is behind our anxiety and learn to deal with the many faces of this phenomenon. This is not a self-help book in the usual sense. For me, performance anxiety is not merely an unpleasant or vexing conditioned reflex we can simply train away by learning various techniques of making a good public impression. The search for our power goes much deeper and lies in the structure of our personality. It has to do not only with the expectations of

9

others and our feelings of inadequacy, but also with deep-seated feelings of anger, shyness, and shame, with an underlying fear of life and of others which is new in our time. As far as I know, this is the first time such a comprehensive attempt has been made in English to delve into the manifold aspects of performance anxiety, with a view towards liberating the power within us.

The fact that I am writing about performance anxiety goes back to a very personal search. Perhaps this book is an attempt to take up the thread of when I was still able to make music light-heartedly and free of fear, or still further back, when as a little "artist" I brought my dolls to life, invented stories, painted pictures, sculpted, and wrote songs. Writing merely at a wise distance I would not be able to make any important pronouncements about performance anxiety. I must have learned about it at first hand; and only by imagining myself in such a position can I now come up with statements that are credible and thus valid. So much for my own motivation and for what stimulated me to approach my own performance anxiety and my love-hate relationship to it, a quality emanating from the dual nature of stage fright itself. Performance anxiety comprises both elements: pleasurable anticipation and fear.

Performance anxiety is not hereditary: it arises from one's own individual experience. How, when, and why it happens to us, or why for some it is like a dormant illness leading to multifaceted symptoms—we still know little about these questions. As far as I can see, its origins lie in our early childhood. A decisively important breeding-ground for stage fright is the "stage set" of school, where we learn very early to understand life as a succession of fear-inspiring situations in which we have to prove ourselves. In school, and often already in kindergarten, we learn the bitter lesson of the more or less pronounced incompatibility of our wishes and our individuality with society's norms. It is here that we learn to be "good", to be "well-behaved", and "well adjusted". Above all: we must be "better than the others", if we are to make a good impression. Our fear of others, of our referees and rivals, is therefore not a mere figment of our imagination. To the contrary, our achievement- and rivalry-oriented institutions of learning are virtual hotbeds of what we call performance anxiety. Here a typical excerpt from a conversation with a school child: "Why don't you want to sing for your class? At home you love to sing." "Because they'd laugh at me."

When we have performance anxiety, then one thing is sure: we are not at ease. On the contrary, we are tight, inhibited, blocked; and our only desire is to flee from the spell of our inner and outer judges, or simply from those who unsettle us with their gaze or their mere presence. When do we have performance anxiety? Why? What kind of feelings does it produce? Can it be overcome, or simply thrown off by an act of will?

In this book I will deal with questions like these, being perfectly aware that this subject has no dazzling or impressive connotations. Whoever is subject to this kind of anxiety is unsuitable for being the center of attention. Whoever merely wishes to swim along at the top will do well to avoid any confrontation with this counterproductive feeling. For such persons—the so-called "cool" ones—I have definitely not written this book.

Authors who devote themselves to the sunny side of our behavior enjoy the advantage of being able to bask a little in the radiance of the object of their portrayal. Such reflected fame is not to be earned with the subject of performance anxiety. Not at all, for here we enter a terrain bristling with warning signs—"Please do not touch", "Do not enter"—as if merely speaking about the subject were to contravene some social tact, as if its very nature were dominated by the stigmata of fear and shame. That there is a curse lying over this subject became quite clear to me during my research for this book. Even modern heroes such as Tina Turner or Justus Frantz were not willing to allow a glimpse into this "dark side" of their and our existence.

It is not surprising, therefore, that the majority of those afflicted are helpless and unenlightened in the face of the problem known as performance anxiety. Even a successful artist such as Pablo Casals, in his book *Talks with Corredor*, admitted to fear before his performances: "Oh, this anxiety, this fear! Never, neither then nor later, could I get rid of it. Believe me: although since then I have given a thousand concerts, I was always just as worked up as the first time... Some of my impending public concerts oppress me like a nightmare. Even today."

A comparison between afflicted persons who are enlightened as to self-help and preventative measures pertaining to performance anxiety and its background, and those who put up with it as a constant chaperon, ensnared in endless exertions even to the end of their lives, shows that it is time to take a caring interest in those who suffer and struggle. It is for these people that this book is written. For them there is hope; for performance anxiety is not an unalterable characteristic of our personality, no inevitable destiny. There are ways and innovative possibilities away from fear and into creative energy and performance power. They are dealt with in the second part of this book.

Perhaps in reading this book you will not encounter anything fundamentally new; but perhaps you will be able to take a closer look at certain traits of your old familiar companion and to see their effects in a new light, so that out of the shadow of your performance anxiety that positive element can emerge which is a possibility hidden in every performance anxiety: pleasurable anticipation. This is one of the keys to our performance power.

Performance Power

PART ONE:
THE MANY FACETS OF
PERFORMANCE
ANXIETY

Performance Power

1

What is Performance Anxiety?

Performance anxiety—or stage fright—is essentially fear of life. It can mean either a depressing burden or a heightening tingle of the nerves. Except in certain extreme cases it is a healthy reaction to situations fraught with risk, because in every situation in which we expose ourselves, we run the risk of making ourselves ridiculous or of failing entirely. It is, then, merely an understandable reaction to situations in which we lay ourselves open to the judgment of those around us—a challenge for which hardly any of us has ever been prepared.

It is just before going onstage. We have gotten ready, we've put on our finest outfit, and we're checking our appearance in the mirror for the last time before going to that place where, today, we will stand in the limelight. The audience is slowly finding its way to its seats... And suddenly it is there: that funny feeling at the pit of our stomach. And those cold hands, and then the catastrophic visions... "What shall I do if my memory slips, if my voice breaks, if my hands tremble, if I fail? Dear Lord, I'd just as soon call it all off. How did I ever come to accept something like this, to feel myself capable of doing this? If the people

17

only knew..."

Whoever reads these lines and feels himself addressed knows what I am writing about: performance anxiety, or stage fright. Nearly everyone is familiar with it, almost all of us have experienced it at least once in our lives. All of us at one time or another have been or can become victims of performance anxiety. We are not alone with it. On the contrary: as privately as this phenomenon may manifest itself, it is just as universal. In the last analysis, everyone who shows himself in public to his fellows in any way at all—be it by speaking, negotiating, acting, dancing, participating in sports, making music—opens himself up to this condition. It always blocks our path just then when we want to show the courage of revealing ourselves or expressing ourselves to our peers. Performance anxiety, then, has something to do with our showing ourselves with our various possibilities of expression to others, thus allowing an insight into our personality. Every public utterance is at the same time self-revelation: we give ourselves away, whether we like it or not.

Social situations of a public nature are the true breeding-grounds of performance anxiety, for this affliction does not flourish in splendid isolation. Its roots are in an environment of references to and relationships with others. When we reveal ourselves through our creations, ideas, or products, these others—they may be invisible—are always present in our memory, our thoughts, and our hearts, even though we may not be conscious of them. In every act of expression we are confronted with other people, groups, or societies that we have made a part of our subconscious. Our stage fright does not exist in a vacuum, therefore, but under the gaze and in the ears of others, be they subconscious or real, compassionate, critical, or punishing.[1]

Performance anxiety or stage fright is almost

universally defined as a state of restlessness, marked by fear and psycho-vegetative tension, before and even during a performance. Hartmann gave an extensive description of that state in 1982: "Stage fright describes a condition of agitation and fear through which a person's capacity for achievement is impaired, a condition which arises before or when a person performs alone or non-anonymously in front of an audience by acting, speaking, singing, or playing an instrument, or wishes to or is supposed to produce a result which is either assessable or is to be assessed, whereby this person's feelings of self-worth can be strongly aroused. Fear and agitation always go along with physiological reactions of the body (clammy hands, strong heart palpitation, cramped muscles, etc.), the so-called stress reaction... This experience, once made, leads inevitably to a second fear, namely, fear of the stage fright, the fear of trembling, sweating, or also having a memory lapse."[2]

The synonym for performance anxiety, "stage fright" (Ger. *Lampenfieber*, literally, footlight fever) is an adaptation of the older term "cannon fright" (*Kanonenfieber*, cannon fever) and does not occur before 1858.[*page 20] It originated in the world of the theater. There the footlights were called the limelight, produced by the burning of lime. In our present-day usage the word "stage fright" is applied not only to the world of the theater, but to all the areas of our social life where we perform, are in the limelight, go "onstage". Regardless of whether we are young or old, pupil or teacher, student or professor, we all can be affected thereby—and we are, too, more or less, when we put ourselves in a situation in which we have to reveal ourselves to others on any one of the many stage sets of our social lives, be it the stadium, the school, college, or university, the shoptable, the concert hall, the world stage or the stage of community politics, the opera house or jam session, the lecture hall or conference room.

---

* I found the oldest reference to how to cope with performance anxiety in Johann Joachim Quantz's *Essay at an Introduction to Playing the Transverse Flute (Versuch einer Anleitung die Flöte traversiere zu spielen)* from the year 1752. He writes (p. 168): "If a flutist who wants to perform in public is fearful and not yet used to playing in the presence of many persons, he should try while playing to direct his attention only to the music that he has in front of him, and never to cast his eyes on those present: for in so doing his thoughts will become distracted, and his composure will be lost. Let him not undertake such difficult pieces which he never succeeded in playing while practising alone, but let him hold to those which he can toss off at a whim. Anxiety gives rise to convulsions of the blood, whereby the lungs are brought into unequal movement and the fingers and tongue come into heat as well. From this condition a trembling of the limbs inevitably follows, one which is quite obstructive to playing the instrument; and the flutist will neither be capable of playing long passages in one breath, nor will he be able to master particular difficulties as he could with a calm spirit. In addition, it will probably happen under such circumstances, especially during warm weather, that he begins to sweat at the mouth; and the flute thereby no longer remains lying firmly in its proper place, but gradually slips downwards; whereby the mouth-hole becomes too covered up and the tone at least too weak, if indeed it does not fail entirely. In order quickly to remedy this last misfortune, let the flutist wipe his mouth and the flute off clean and then grasp into his hair, that is, his wig, rubbing the fine powder clinging to his fingers onto his mouth. Hereby the sweat pores will be clogged, and he will be able to continue playing without further hindrance."

Let us examine the term equivalent to stage fright or performance anxiety more closely: "footlight fever". The term "footlight" signifies that we are lit up by an artificial light source. We are illuminated, spotlighted, we are standing in the limelight. Our body reacts to this exposure with increased warmth or arousal, a mobilization of the body's own defenses against the stress induced by the footlights. We become heated up, "fever"-ish in the fight against the intruder "footlight" who wishes despotically to conquer territory within us for himself. As with all feverish illnesses, the following applies: when the intruder has invaded us completely, the only remedy is to let him do as he pleases—to let go—in order to let the fever reach its climax, so as to use the energy of the feverish heat to begin a new phase of refinding ourselves.

It seems instructive after this short digression that performance anxiety's *alter ego*, "footlight fever", does not only signify that particular psychic stress induced by public performance, as is held in general opinion today; it also designates the accompanying pleasurable, exciting component. The phenomenon of performance anxiety, stage fright, footlight fever, or whatever we wish to call it, is Janus-faced. On the one hand, it can be experienced as a state of arousal, a positive stimulus leading to increased watchfulness, to more intensive concentration, and thus to improved performance, and on the other, as an inhibiting or braking force blocking our efficiency.

In the many conversations and interviews I have carried out concerning performance anxiety, it has been revealing for me to learn which associations the term awakens individually, how positive or negative its semantic components are, and which positive or negative attributions come up. My insight grew: unpleasant experiences with past situations tend to get glued like labels to new situations, leading to virtual programming of performance anxiety. It does not matter if such a coupling of old and new is a result of our own actions, an effect of external circumstances, or simply a pleasurable inconvenience. Years of collective research on our phenomenon have produced an insight as simple as the well-known proverb which formulates it even more succinctly: a burned child shuns the fire.

Performance anxiety can mean either a depressing burden or a heightening tingle of the nerves. Except in certain extreme cases it is not an illness, but a healthy reaction to situations fraught with risk, because in every situation in which we expose ourselves, we run the risk of making ourselves look ridiculous or of failing entirely. It is, then, merely an understandable reaction to situations in which we lay ourselves open to the judgment of those around us—a challenge for which hardly any of us has ever been prepared. Whether we regard our own personal performance anxiety positively, as a means of increasing our efficiency and finding our performance power, or negatively, as fraught with fear and shame—it always has the connotation of our being evaluated by a more or less anonymous audience, regardless of how large or small. It thrives on the stage set of interpersonal relations.

Choosing between the various synonyms "performance anxiety", "footlight fever", and "stage fright", I have chosen the former, because it tells us we are dealing with a multifaceted phenomenon. It is a feeling associated not just with acting on the stage set of a theater, but one having to do with a much larger one: the social stage. We are all actors on the social stage. It is here that our fears and anxieties have their place. Whether they are justified or not, necessary or not, insuperable or not—we will learn more in the next chapter.

Instead of the Limelight—Just for Fun

In our private performances without an audience we are free of performance anxiety, because evaluation from outside is missing. Persons who do not "put their light under a bushel" and show themselves in public expose themselves to situations that can be psychologically explosive.

Public performances are expected to be perfect, aesthetically pleasing, meaningful, or just beautiful—thus the expectations to which persons performing in public subject themselves. Not everybody wishes to appear in public before an audience. Many people prefer to try out their capabilities and skills in private, for their own pleasure. I am thinking here about the many persons who live out their ambitions as dancers or singers at home, who deliver important speeches or perform acts of daring in front of the mirror, without ever presenting them to an audience. They enjoy their activity without an outward stimulus, simply out of pleasure at the activity itself, without any need for recognition, applause, or criticism.

We are all familiar with such situations, in which we act out our capabilities and skills for ourselves alone, out of pure pleasure. Private performances can reveal how much we can do, how much we have practised and learned, and how we are able to rise to certain challenges. In such settings, we learn to assess and to understand ourselves. We come to know our potential for improvement, our limits, and our possibilities. As under the looking-glass we encounter our self or parts of it; and in so doing, we experience who we really are or who we are about to become. In so doing, we are not only performers, but also our own critics. We appraise ourselves, and we create our own motivation and encouragement to continue. We also define ourselves according to our own standards, without for a moment asking what others are thinking about us.

Performances of this kind serve the end of self-fulfillment. This type of self-representation is completely sufficient and satisfactory for many persons. They need no outside motivation and do not need to stand in the public limelight. It is enough for them to derive pleasure from their play and to enjoy proving their capabilities to themselves alone. They need no audience, for they fulfil all the requirements by themselves: they are performer and audience in one. As a rule, such persons are also free of performance anxiety. Why? Because an important prerequisite is missing: evaluation from outside.

We find private performances of this kind with all healthy children. They make up songs, dance, mimic, write poetry, create theater pieces and roles, and play with dolls. During the course of their development, these possibilities of expression can be developed, or they can be impeded and suppressed. In any case, it is striking that we seldom find adolescents and especially grownups displaying this type of behavior. Is this because older people simply pursue such activities less frequently, or is it more difficult for them to see such play as a praiseworthy form of activity as such? Is it a sign of our times that we recognize and attach high importance only to activities taking place in the public eye? Speaking in the jargon of our age: is it only something that "gets me something" that counts?

This little excursion into the realm of private performances without which our world would be much the poorer should make clear that there are private utterances and statements which produce very little or no performance anxiety, and that there are persons for whom this kind of private sampling of their personalities is perfectly sufficient.

However, we wish to deal with those persons who do not "put their light under a bushel", who have the courage or the need to reveal themselves in public, and who thereby expose themselves to situations of self-expression that can be psychologically explosive.

You can easily see what I mean if you imagine that you have to give a little speech at some kind of celebration. You stand up, every eye is upon you, all of a sudden you can hear a pin drop. You take a deep breath and begin, at first with some restraint, then with an increasingly secure voice... An astute observer would not fail to notice certain bodily transformations you went through in these first moments—a slight trembling, nervous hands, a subtle restlessness of the legs... Perhaps you, too, will ascertain that your self-perception suddenly changes, discovering a certain feeling of agitation as soon as you find yourself at the center of attention.

Again and again I have found that the mere words "public performance" by themselves can cause feelings of restlessness, embarrassment, or defensiveness. In fact, it costs energy and courage to show oneself in public. The anxious question, "How do I look to others?", cannot simply be put aside, no matter how gracious and wise we may appear to be.

Nor can this question be dismissed as a mere neurotic reaction. On the contrary: in a world in which appearances mean everything and authenticity next to nothing, in a world in which, in public, one meets only beautiful, busy, efficient, and self-confident persons—in such a world there is no place for feelings, neither for oneself nor for others. It is characteristic of such a world that we hold disturbing feelings at arm's length, encouraged by a flood of books hawking sermons of success, that we train our "lightness of being", not to be brought off balance by anyone or anything. In such a world, fear and performance anxiety are in a tough position, for we would much rather attribute such feelings to brooders and problematic characters. Whoever wishes to swim along at the top cannot allow himself feelings like these, but must avoid going into the depths, not becoming irritated or distracted by inefficient feelings.

Whether we like it or not, however, these feelings do exist and demand our attention. Whoever is ready to come to terms with them and their inner meaning will be forced first of all to deal with their background, since these feelings are neither enigmatic black beasts nor an inevitable destiny. They have causes and reasons which are rooted in the humus of our society.

Conditio humana: The Person in the Limelight and His Audience

As opposed to the setting of spontaneous happenings, a participant in a performance is burdened with expectations. He is left completely alone, however, when it comes to how he deals with the pressure of expectations and their consequences.

In order to illuminate the background of performance anxiety, let us for a moment investigate what sets performances in front of an audience apart from the mainstream of human happenings. Performances are social situations deriving their significance from the presence and participation of observers. It is expected of performances that they effect an experience in others. The actor or performer must capture the observers' attentive eye and ear, he or she must arouse interest and create pleasure. The spectators wish to be transported from a position of cool observation into a condition in which they become spellbound, swept along, or fascinated. Therefore, it is not sufficient that such an event be carried out technically correctly or faultlessly; beyond that it should somehow be interesting, absorbing, or impressive. Technical perfection, to be sure, creates satisfaction, but it does not leave a lasting impression of remarkability in the memories of the participating observers. Let us think of how a crowd is swept along by an exciting, elegantly played ballgame or by the shooting of the decisive goal. The spectators are there to enjoy, wish to be moved, and also desire—besides a feeling of contentment—to take pleasure in an aesthetic experience.

Every performance is communication, because it is also expresses a message. It allows participation in meanings, situations, and experiences shared by human beings and also bestows experiences on the participating observers or listeners. Boundaries separating people from one another become razed, creating participation and partnership. The moment of aesthetic experience, however, does not appear until the material is treated in such a way that it becomes the activating, stimulating stuff of a new experience. Continuity, intensity, concentration, excitement, vitality—these are some of the criteria a performance is expected to fulfil. In addition, whether we are dealing with a speech, a concert, or a sports event, it is always a matter of a balance between maintenance of the past on the one hand, thus creating familiarity, and renewal on the other, thus advancing progress. Too much familiarity as well as too much renewal arouse an audience's resistance. The person in the limelight is expected to cultivate continuance of values and feelings as well as solidarity and confirmation of norms, but also to offer the impetus for something new to emerge. The audience, on the one hand and in order to take part, wishes to see itself represented or reflected, but at the same time it also wishes to participate in the living-out of unrehearsed possibilities, yearnings, and desires represented by the person in the limelight.[3]

Every performance bears in itself an element of the epiphany. One or more performers step out of their invisibility and unveil themselves into perceptibility, the audience being witnesses. The persons so revealing themselves are made to be more than they are in reality: they become elevated and are made to be significant. They are shown respect and admiration, because they become raised above the masses and are conspicuous. The relation of audience to performer is one of bartering, one in which emotional goods are exchanged. The audience pays with esteem and receives a confirmation of its own importance in return. Performances provide a stage set for such exchanges, in that they contribute through time, place, decoration, and cast of characters towards the performers' being separated from the spectators, mystified and stylized.

As opposed to spontaneous manifestations, in performances the participants' roles are predefined and prestructured. Thus in keeping with the power and prestige at stake, a performer is burdened with expectations. It is here that the individual finds himself in a problematic situation, for he is thrust into a specific role which, to be sure, may contain some elements of satisfaction, but also offers definite elements of repression. The individual is left completely alone when it comes to how he deals with the compulsion to success, the pressure of expectations, and their consequences.[4]

The stratification present in every performance— something being acted out in front of the eyes and ears of others, whereby something else is also produced, that is, contact, coming together, or relationship—is also present in every situation in which a number of human beings is involved. Performances therefore represent not only condensed human events, but also the situation of human society itself. Collective conceptions are exposed to view, thereby acquiring an element of spectacularity—that is, they arouse attention. The well-known saying, "Justice must not only be done, it must be seen to be done", makes this clear. What this means is that it is not enough that justice exists or is lived out; it must also be made visible and be demonstrated to mankind. It does not suffice us, then, to know that some persons are more gifted for sports or for music than others; we also want to see it acted out before our eyes, in order to be able to participate. These persons do something for us which we all would like to have, where we all would like to be. They are elevated above the masses—and we with them.

Those "heroes" who lend our daily routine wings, or at least food for conversation, always arrive at a certain point, despite their virtuosity in repression: fear is taboo! No audience is interested in fear. On the contrary: we try to exterminate it by life- and body-styling. Traces of cold sweat are regarded with embarrassment, but sooner or later some company will come up with a neutralizing deodorant.* My question is, though: How long can we go on playing make-believe?

---

* It was this ironical sentence—as if there ever could be such a thing as a deodorant against perspiration caused specifically by fear—written in the German edition of this book (1993) which garnered me my first invitation by a large cosmetics company to give a seminar on performance anxiety at a press conference ... on the occasion of their

launching a new deodorant onto the market! It was my introduction to High Society, so to speak. Discretion forbids me to make a statement about that deodorant's properties against the underlying fear behind the perspiration.

Socio-Cultural Background

With the gradual disappearance in significance of the material world and the increasing importance of virtual and visual elements in our lives, the phenomenon of performance anxiety proves to be a last remnant of authentic reality generally hidden away from an applauding public.

How an individual deals with his performance anxiety represents in a certain way a reflection of how we are trying today to cope with our fear in general, or to flee from it. Only if we perceive the individual in and within his world, together with his roles, relationships, ties, and troubles, can we begin to understand personal suffering and collective misery in their reciprocity. Hasty pragmatism and a screening out of the mutual binding of an individual and his world—two qualities we find time and again in the many "how-to" books available today—may perhaps facilitate a concrete intervention in an individual case, but they do not contribute to a discovery of the causes behind the causes. What such books transmit is the illusion that performance anxiety can be trained or therapied away, and that for every symptom there is an expert who can somehow quantify or otherwise cope pragmatically with our problems with fear. The consequence of such a superficial approach means that before we have really taken a closer look at our fear of spectators and taken a stand against it, we have already pushed it aside or reduced it to an assessable concrete problem behind which, in my opinion, a much larger existential fear is looming.

In other words, when we have performance anxiety we have a choice. We can take a quick fix, as it were, read a self-help book, learn some tricks, and alter some symptom or other, or we can perceive the situation as an opportunity to change, and go into the matter more deeply. In the first case, we will not get rid of the "glue" all over our body which continues to attach us to mama and papa and all those authorities out there vying for our attention and our subservience. In the second case, we will go through a process of transformation, at the end of which we will not require these other persons. We will have become our own self and discovered our true power. Such a process can be frightening, however, and we have to be ready for such a change.

Our performance anxiety is like a mirror showing us where we stand in life. According to Dale Carnegie, the fear of showing oneself in public is at the top of the list of one's fears, the fear of death, for example, only occupying seventh place.

It is not by accident that we can read again and again that we are living in an age of fear. A glance at my own practice confirms this fact, for at least half of my patients has problems of fear. Disturbances concerned with fear are so widespread that scholars are speaking of a psycho-social epidemic. A vast flood of publications on this subject, and the fact that fear-calming medications are the most frequently prescribed remedies today, only confirm this gloomy impression.

The specific character or essence of fear in our time derives not as in former times from the unreckonable, untamed force of nature but from the *fear of other persons.*

This particular kind of fear consorts with transformations in the power structure of present-day society. It is specifically because today for the first time in history we are imaginable as single individuals (and less as representatives of our station in society). We thus have the possibility of being somehow different and distinct from others, and for each one of us the Other begins to take on a greater importance. Just as the medieval concept of one's ties between the self, the world, and others has dissolved, for the individual a feeling of separateness, demarcation, or estrangement from others is now coming into the foreground. Whoever does not know his identity is at least wishing to be different. What is in short supply, individuates—and that in the last analysis is what everybody wants.[5]

With the gradual disappearance in significance of the material world and the increasing importance of virtual and visual elements in our lives, human interrelationships thereby appearing essentially as imaginary ones, the phenomenon of performance anxiety proves to be a last remnant of individuality which defies socialization. It is a remnant of authentic reality generally hidden away from an applauding public. Put in positive terms: it is a defense against society's disciplining, or actually a remnant of reality which has been pushed behind the scenes and which, from that vantage-point, proves to be inhibiting and ambivalent. Performance anxiety may not be subjugated to immediate sanctions, but it is all the more massively enslaved to personal feelings of shame and guilt.

In our time, people spend long hours daily in imaginary worlds, looking at TV, videos, and films, listening to music, playing computer games. The result of this is that most people are hardly capable of feeling insight or enlightenment directly any more. They also have great difficulty in expressing emotions in real life. Instead, they experience them in imaginary realms, thus becoming estranged to themselves and others.[6] I have also noticed in my practice that children with digital watches—not like the "old-fashioned" ones where one can see the hour and minute hands by their sweep expressing the passage of time—have the greatest difficulty in feeling what time is. For them, time is not an element that is flowing; it is just a number.

This lack of authenticity leads to a loss of reality and with it of autonomy. The result is a heightened dependence on the judgment of the Other. We are finding ourselves today in a mirroring stage, one in which each of us is thrown back on himself and on his merely phantasied relationship to the Other, whose power is imagined. The power attributed to the Other rests only partially on real experiences with him, resulting above all from internalized norms and fears.

With both our glance and our self-definition mirrored in the Other, aesthetic categories, too, take on another meaning. During the Renaissance era the sense of the visual was a subordinate one, but in our time it has advanced into the center. We are now living under the spell of mirrors, writes Lasch.[7] The mirrors are the eyes of the others; and in this world, bewitched by images, in which those senses responsible for nearness—touching and contacting—are withering up, it is hardly surprising, even consistent with the pattern, that our life is becoming more and more closely related to the art of acting. We play-act for others and finally for ourselves as well, until first the others and eventually we too believe in our game.

The weakening of the senses responsible for nearness and the vanishing of the warm forces of feeling are only one disastrous result of a process which has been going on for a long time: the retreat of reality from our lives. This has led to a situation in which illusion and make-believe are everything. In the same measure as the world which can be experienced directly is shrinking away from us, we become more and more estranged from each other and from ourselves, and the world takes on the aspect of a huge unfathomable cauldron of danger. To be cool is "in", even if we thereby freeze. Social situations become test situations, inspections as it were, in which a not inconsiderable part of our energy is diverted to the warding-off of fear. Moreover, it is just this warding-off which leaves us confronted more than ever with two prerational fears which we feel we must fend off at any price: the fears of embarrassment and of loss of reputation.

However, the battle against the chief enemy—fear—cannot be won. No matter how much we kick and bite, we can only fend off the enemy temporarily; for fear is a life-preserving mechanism. If we want to emerge from the vicious circle of the mirrors, we will then have to remove the spectacles of materialistic perception and learn to view others and ourselves as human beings with weaknesses and shortcomings.

One of the tasks of our time, therefore, is once again to give feelings and personal elements their due. Showing respect for our vulnerability and owning up to our errors and weaknesses could serve as guiding principles for a society which would expressly allow its members to behave in ways which they cannot change anyway.

2

"All the World's a Stage"

We are all interconnected by way of our roles in the game we play on the big stage set of life. Theater roles and daily roles may have different consequences in reality, but both require the same techniques and props. Both run the risk of sudden exposure.

When the catch phrase "stage fright" is uttered, all sorts of terms from the world of the theater turn up in free association: role, scene, piece, stage set. "All the world's a stage"—"Our life is a drama"—"We are all play-acting"— *Theatrum mundi*: these are all familiar phrases that may even seem a little worn, but they actually correspond to basic human experience. From antique times up to the present day we can continually find metaphors of the theater used to describe human life. If in earlier times it was the gods into whose hands human beings were delivered up, today it is society's dictation of roles and expectations that we have to fill or fulfil.[9] What used to be attributed to external forces now falls back on us alone.

In our daily language we can find numerous metaphors of the stage set: "show off", "play-act", "put on an act", "act the part", "act up", "play the role", "fall out of

35

the role", "depart from the script", "exchange roles", etc. They prove that the language of the theater is descriptive of many of our daily experiences. If we realize that the word "person" originally meant "mask", we must thereby acknowledge that everywhere we look, all of us are more or less consciously playing a role, are more or less consciously onstage. An examination of the metaphors of the stage set mentioned above reveals strikingly that they all are employed to denote states of make-believe. These expressions tend to have negative connotations and are often used as a foil for what we perceive to be reality. The question is, however, whether a well-acted scene is not in itself a kind of reality, and whether it isn't a kind of reality when someone plays his role to perfection or when a certain role seems to have been written with us so much in mind that it becomes second nature to us. On the other hand, we know that there is a difference between theater roles and so-called daily ones. A theater role is an illusion and does not have the same ramifications as in daily life, where our roles have genuine consequences: something can happen to us. However, what theater and daily roles have in common is the fact that both require real techniques. Both use masks and standardized props, and both run the risk of sudden exposure.[10]

Our Roles

The protective and defense maneuvers that we have built up to fortify the impression we make on others may give us a certain security, but they cannot affect the radiation which we emit.

Ever since we were small, roles and models of roles have been played out in front of us, showed to us, and required of us. We are assigned good and poor roles, useful and useless ones. Sometimes we are forced into a particular role. Sometimes of our own free will we take over someone else's role, and by imitation are able to melt it into our own repertoire of roles. Every person has a repertoire of the roles he is able to play, as well as a stock of those he has already played at some time or other; these are all engraved into our memory.[11] The capability of personifying roles is pre-existing, is built into our body and soul. From the very moment of birth, our body and soul become endowed with basic capabilities of imitation, spontaneity, and communication.[12] Those roles we are capable of personifying, and the scenes and sequences we have known—all are stored away in the archives of our body and soul. It is through them that we experience our particular feeling of "being in the world", a feeling which accomplishes itself within a spectrum which can range from complete adaptation to being an autistic individual completely shut off from others. In this connection, Petzold has emphasized that the "body" as the place of embodiment is not only the material, private body (in the way we say, "my body"), but always the socially affected one ("social body") as well.[13] Our self is thus never merely a "private" one, but always has a "public" component in addition.

Behind the role, a further dimension can be found: the personality, with which we embody a role and thereby transcend it.[14] Through the means of our personality we have the choice—among those roles offered to us and which unite us with society—of which ones we wish to embody, and to what degree. Through our own roles, all of us are united with other role-bearers in a game on the grand stage of life. Whether our preferred place of action is on the stage or in the audience, no matter whether we are actor or audience: we are always "onstage".

Society's expectations invariably express themselves in the form of concrete role models. However, here lie the roots of potential conflict, one revolving around the question as to how individual creativity and societal pressures can be balanced out. Formulated in another way, it is the issue of how our personal search for meaning can be imbedded in the context of society, without our losing ourselves therein or vanishing away to nothingness, but also without society assigning to us from the beginning the role of the "disturbance".[15]

From role theory we know that roles are always configurative. That is, one role determines another. Actors are the way they are, because the public is the way it is; the public is the way it is, because the actor is the way he is—a reciprocal assigning of expectations. Here, too, lies the source of role conflicts, resulting from irreconcilable demands and expectations. Take the example of a woman who is simultaneously mother, housewife, and worker, and who discovers that her various roles cannot be reconciled with one another. Another source of conflict are role expectations which clash with one's own sense of values. As an example I am thinking of musicians who are required to perform works which do not conform to their own personal taste, or whose job requires them to play under mediocre conductors. As a third source of conflict we can mention role expectations which bring an overtaxing of one's capabilities. This means that we can be confronted with an array of responsibilities demanding more of us than we are able to deliver in the required amount of time. We may also be exposed to unclear expectations or evaluations of the job to be done, resulting in real or imaginary sanctions if we fail.

When we deliver a lecture, play a concerto, or sell a

product, we slip into a particular role. We want to transmit a particular image of our personality; we want to be taken seriously. The necessary harmony of all the aspects of our performance points to a basic discrepancy between our self and the image of our personality that we represent to our audience. As personalities in front of an audience, we tend to sketch a figurative portrait of ourselves which is intended to impress. For this reason we veil or bring out certain traits, we hide the discrepancy between our feelings and our comportment. As actors, speakers, etc., in any public performing situation, we are the target of projections of all kinds. That is, we are like a screen onto which our spectators project their expectations, their wishes, and their unfulfilled desires. However, we, the actors, also project expectations, threats, etc., originating in our own personality structures. For instance, we can think that the audience is hostile towards us—in reality a pure projection of our own inner, hostile attitude. In our acting, playing, or whatever, we make use of protective and defense maneuvers in order to shield our projections from others or to preserve the projections of others. In other words: these maneuvers seem necessary to us because the impression of reality awakened by a performance is extremely fragile. One note in the wrong key can destroy the sound of an entire concerto, one fumble can change the outcome of an entire ballgame.

The matter becomes still more uncomfortable when we realize that our communication is only in part subject to our control. To be sure, we can manipulate our words and their content, but the general impression which we give, through our body language, for example, is a matter over which we have little power. The protective and defense maneuvers which we have built up to fortify the impression we wish to make on others can give us a certain sense of security, but they cannot affect the radiation which we emit.

Here a fundamental asymmetry of every "performance" is revealed. As actors or performers, we are aware only of the stream of our communication. The spectators, however, can perceive a second stream of communication: radiation which we send out through our body. To think that we have our own "private sphere" is thus a pretty illusion, for our audience can actually read from our radiation what is going on inside us.

When you communicate, be aware that the actual words you say make up only ten to twenty per cent of your message! The lion's share of the message perceived by the audience consists of another kind of language which is international, even universal: body language. This is the only kind of communication which cannot lie. We can adjust all the details of our delivery, but we cannot "style" our inner feelings. Through our body language, they come across much more clearly to our audience than what we think we are communicating.

How would you react, dear reader, in the following situation? You have just listened to a brilliantly styled speech, as far as language, the right jokes at the right time, etc., are concerned. The speaker had the right tie on, and he even gave a passionate commitment to his theme. Afterwards you go backstage to congratulate the speaker on his brilliant delivery and his commitment, and he gives you his hand. It is cold. What do you think now about his commitment? (Deduction: his brain was committed, but not his heart!)

It is interesting to note that every society has a well-developed interest in disturbances or incongruities in this area. The repository of stories about embarrassing situations, revelations, or observations seems infinitely large when we realize how many gatherings have been enlivened by such tales as a source of amusement, of malicious joy,...

or as an expression of fear and apprehension.

Performance Anxiety and Role

Let us remain with role theory for a moment and illuminate the phenomenon of performance anxiety from that perspective. With every performance, we perceive role expectations from two sides: from inside ourselves and from the point of view of others. From our personal attitude towards a given role—"it fits me like a glove", or "this role does not come easily to me"—our specific way of approaching a role is formed. Our feeling of self-worth is moulded by the roles we take on, by our attitudes to them, and by the esteem in which they are held from outside. If we do not feel at ease in a particular role or hold it in low esteem, our feeling of self-worth suffers. It also suffers when we become plagued with apprehensions of not being able to play a certain role adequately, and from there it is only a small step until we become unsure of ourselves.

Performance situations are often a mixture of attraction and avoidance. On the one hand we are fascinated by seeing and being seen—a challenge to our ego—and on the other, we are afraid of being exposed, of possible embarrassment, and sometimes even of success. As if under a spell from these ambivalent feelings, we thus do not find ourselves in a position to determine clearly if we should accept a given role with all its consequences or if we should throw it aside and forge ahead. We freeze in indecision ... and this is the point at which fear sets in. Our energy can no longer flow unhindered, since it has become sucked in by this conflict, the message of which often reads: "I want to show myself and win recognition, but I'd rather hide", or "I don't enjoy continually playing the boss, but I get so much attention from doing so".

This kind of conflict also arises when we are compelled constantly to repeat sequences of a role. Even if a role gives pleasure at the beginning, the length of time during which a person can endure playing it over and over again is limited. Actors and musicians, especially, are befallen by the phenomenon of "role fatigue", because evening for evening, subject to the same routine, they are expected not to show their saturation.[16] They are even expected to play each time as if it were for the first time. My organ teacher once gave me the wise advice: "Don't ever play a piece for more than three months." I believe that he discovered a basic truth.

The less our public roles are compatible with our private ones and the more our public roles reduce or even cripple us, the larger looms the danger of damage to our personality. Conflicts with our co-actors and with our audience are also connected with such incompatibility. With some persons, the wish to "look good" to their colleagues and partners creates a certain tension which leads to their feeling of being a lonesome soldier fighting a solitary battle on an isolated battlefield, a feeling such persons develop so as to avoid humiliation. Often they do not allow others to participate in their preparation of a role because they are apprehensive of their malicious joy, their envy, or their cynicism. Rather go it alone than be seen by others as weak or somehow at fault, these "lonesome soldiers" think.

The same is true of our conflict with the audience. It can take on destructive aspects if we constantly expect ourselves to be in top form, to come up with something new, to improve ourselves still more, or to stand in an ever better light.

The chief conflict, however, lies in the fact that, according to its etymology, a role is bound up with a more or less conserved or "canned" comportment. Depending on how rigid, narrowly defined, or frozen a role is, our resistance to it increases. The more we are led away from ourselves by predetermined roles, the greater our resistance, as well as our susceptibility to the fears of insufficiency or failure. Illustrations of this syndrome are provided by actors or classical musicians, whose pieces and scores are fixed. However, looking at other social stereotypes—gypsy or jazz musicians, or doctors and judges—we find much less anxiety, because these people are allowed a certain spontaneity.

At the other end of the role spectrum we find the extemporaneous role games of children, whose creations are allowed to be free and spontaneous. Whether they play Indians, cops and robbers, racing drivers, or presidents, they trust their own imagination and ideas and are thus free from resistance or fear of expectations.

In sum, performance anxiety is linked to the degree in which a given role is perceived to be strange to one's self. The danger of performance anxiety increases almost in direct proportion to the rigidity and limiting qualities of a role which hardly allows an individual any degree of freedom.

Now that all this has been said, what can we extract from it for our behavior with performance anxiety? To me, the heart of the matter seems to be that we have spent at least the first two decades of our lives as learners and recipients, within a group of learners or listeners. Thus we have practised listening and receiving. Finding ourselves now as adults in the position of the giver, the lecturer, or the teacher, we suddenly discover that we have learned only inadequately to perform this transformation. We possess no expertise at coping with the changed circumstances of the lecturer's role, for example; for this role demands other capabilities and skills than those we have practised assiduously in the daily routine of life. Appearing in public demands a changed state of consciousness and altered attention, the rules of which we must be familiar with in order to perform the metamorphosis to a leading or giving role. Above all we must be able to perceive our role with full concentration. This implies our recognition of having something to say and that we stand alone, with no other choice than to bring our presentation to a close, once started. There is no retreat, no "not yet", no *mañana*. When the airplane takes off, it has to land as well.

When we have finally discovered which requirements a role as giver, lecturer, teacher, or performer demands of us, we can then take a step forward and deal with the ways in which we wish to enliven and transform our role. In other words: how can we fill the jar of role expectations with personal content? Instead of becoming the jam, we should become the canner!—this should be our goal, one which challenges us to discover our own spontaneity, to have the courage to experiment, or even to take the risk of defining our expectations of a role anew.

Role and Personality

Without a theory of personality it is not possible to answer the question: what leads to the kind of personality able to deal constructively with the energy of performance anxiety?

Every understanding and every treatment of performance anxiety has to have in its background the idea of what defines human beings and how personality emerges, is made up, and functions. Without a theory of personality we cannot answer the question: what leads to a healthy personality? Or, seen in the light of our subject: what leads to the kind of personality able to deal constructively with the energy mobilized by performance anxiety?

The metaphors appearing again and again in connection with performance anxiety, such as "the others see me in such-and-such a way", or "I make a picture of myself", contain ideas of personality embedded in our culture. Not all cultures are familiar with these particular metaphors, and during the course of history our metaphors, too, have gradually become changed. Personality as we understand it today simply did not exist back in those days when people lived in hordes or in groupings according to station. It was only during the Renaissance that something like a personal biography arose. Only then did artists begin to sign their works, did scientists begin to make a name for themselves, and as far as architecture is concerned, did the separation of private from public rooms take place. The meaning of personal possessions, or of personal distinction through clothing, the art of cooking, or of living, began to be felt only then. The ensuing separation of the individual from the group finally resulted in his activity appearing as something for which he alone was responsible or which he alone attained. Today, with human beings being thrown back on themselves, performance anxiety, too, has come to acquire a larger dimension, one in which the formation of personality or identity moves more strongly, though not exclusively, into the foreground.

How does personality develop? Or, how does identity unfold? Two crucial components are body and soul, and the ego. Body and soul as an expression of a person's totality is the foundation of that which is defined as the individual's "self". Everything happening to us—our luck, our pleasure, our injuries, and our distress—is stored in our body and soul. In the expression of our eyes, in the "rubber tire" around our middle, in the "crow's feet" at the corner of our eyes, and in the virtual imprint of our memory, the scenes we have experienced are preserved, gaining power for new scenes. Herein lies the nature of socialization: we internalize roles, scenes, and pieces and with them atmospheres, impressions, and feelings which we have experienced in the company of others.

At the same time, however, our body and soul can also become a potential place of repression. This happens as soon as we estrange ourselves from our bodily impulses. The price we pay for this estrangement is high, for bodily impulses thus degenerate to symptoms, the signs of alienated corporeality. An example of such estrangement is the escalating credence we give to physical fitness as a decisive criterion of the quality of life. Just look at the jogger, sworn to a program which he feels he must absolve and bearing a fierce expression on his face, in comparison to someone sprinting through the woods, who is merely running for enjoyment. Both are in motion, but the difference is crucial. The jogger is absolving a "body program", while the runner in the woods is simply enjoying his feeling of well-being and his corporeality as the foundation of his human existence.

With the growing maturity of the bodily functions and the accompanying learning processes on the motoric, emotional, social, and cognitive levels, the ego is formed. This is the place of conscious perception of the self and conscious action. The ego perceives who or how I am, as opposed to the self, which perceives that I am. The ego recognizes the self, or expressed in reverse: through the ego, the self is able to recognize itself: "I perceive myself", or "I did that myself". The ego as a perceiving, acting, feeling, and thinking being is capable of reflecting upon the self, perceives the direction in which it is going, and superimposes it with images and conceptions of the self: "I see myself", "I perceive myself". Through this inward perception and the processes of evaluation associated with it, pictures of the self arise which are one source of identity formation.

The other source of identity formation are the attributions of role and the expectations from outside. The picture others have of me, the identifyings or recognitions from outside, are perceived by the ego and superimposed with identifications. With this process, the evaluation from outside which I perceive or anticipate gains a decisive meaning for the development of identity. Identity is always two-faced: I recognize who I am (identification), and I am recognized (identified) by persons in my surroundings as the one whom they always see. The attributions of role coming from outside are just as important for the ego as are the individual embodiment and embellishment of these roles. Negative attributions or expectations have their consequences for identity; they can easily become an aggressor from inside. A typical example: "From him you can't expect much" is internalized to become "I can't make it anyway". Positive expectations have their consequences, too, such as when the public stamps a particular athlete to be its favorite, thereby exerting a pressure which turns into self-pressure uttering itself in the compulsion: "I have to win". Others' hopes then weigh more heavily than one's own wishes or needs.

The double definition of identity requires the ego to come to terms with the Others. It is precisely in discussion with others that we learn to comprehend who we are and why we have become the way we are. This process signifies remembrance and anticipation, role model and role potential. From the natural identity of the small child, via the role-bound identity of the schoolchild, to the mature identity of the adult, we are in a lifelong process of developing new facets of identity. We overcome and integrate old facets, thereby gaining the possibility for our identity to grow and flourish, embedded as it always is, of course, in social encounters, ties, and clashes. It is in this reciprocal process that we come to find our standpoint. The issue is to be with ourselves and with others at the same time. This is how meaning arises.

A theory of identity which represents neither the separation from nor the symbiosis with the community but is integrative, opens new perspectives for our theme. It offers help for people who view every "performance" as a possibility for injury to or loss or invasion of their identities. If we understand "identity" to mean "the lifelong practice of identity", then we are not committed for once and for all to a rigid identity. It is for this reason that it is impossible to give a simple definition of what identity or personality "is", for it is a matter not of a state, but of a lifelong process. In any case, we can give a wide berth to biographical coercions by constantly looking for new meanings, questioning or affirming established patterns, and giving new elements their due.

3

The Phenomenology of Performance Anxiety

Performance anxiety is an extremely complex phenomenon. A comprehensive understanding leads from the phenomenon to its structures.

Now that we have illuminated the socio-cultural and role-theoretical background of performance anxiety, we approach its inner landscape. Data, statistics, and measurements can doubtless be helpful, but for a comprehensive understanding of what goes on inside each individual when he is befallen by performance anxiety, they are not worth much. I therefore fall back on a method called phenomenology, which was introduced at the beginning of the 20th century by Edmund Husserl, a pioneer of modern thinking.[18] Phenomenology leads to "the things themselves" not by measurements, but through the direct personal experience of the senses of each and every one of us.

Everything that transpires within us—thoughts, feelings, plots—has several meanings. These are interwoven and complex, since we are not one-dimensional figures answering to simple, linear, or mechanistic laws. In fact, performance anxiety is an extremely complex phenomenon, comparable to a symphony, in which many motifs, melodies, and rhythms are intertwined. The language of performance anxiety is like music, in which one of the voices within us battles with the others, now quiet and restrained, now shrill and loud. It is a battle ending in reconciliation, in a truce, or implacably. This means that the basic structures of performance anxiety are complex and variable. They are rather a palette of reactions than a single, easily defined event. The chief component of performance anxiety is fear. Nevertheless, more than just fear is involved. What is performance anxiety, then? Instead of a definition, let an example give more information.

How Does Performance Anxiety Manifest Itself?

There is not just *one* performance anxiety; instead there are as many different varieties of it as there are human beings.

"...My heart is pounding up into my throat, I can hardly breathe anymore. My knees are trembling, and my hands are sopping wet. I can't think clearly anymore and am confused. I have the feeling that I'm not up to this situation at all, I feel helpless and abandoned. Now it all comes out, the way I bit off more than I can chew. O shame!"

What this afflicted person is describing is a typical pattern of performance anxiety. This short sequence first begins with a description of bodily reactions, then devolves to cognitive and emotional ones, finishing with a description of behavior. Regarded superficially, the lament so raised contains a palette of unpleasant bodily sensations, as well as depressive and fearful feelings and behavior patterns, all of

which are played out on several levels. If we were to delve deeper into this constellation, we could discover a singularly personal pattern. It is one closely bound up with the person's biography, that is, with the long history of evaluations and devaluations experienced by the person in question.

If I have maintained up to now that everybody

knows what performance anxiety is, now I have to revise this statement to read: "Everybody knows his own individual performance anxiety". There is not just *one* performance anxiety; instead there are as many different varieties of it as there are human beings. Everyone has his own unmistakable anxiety profile. Everyone has his own inner resonances on the corporeal, emotional, and cognitive levels, in his behavior, imagination, and in the realm of remembered scenes.

To an observer standing at a distance, the inherent meaningfulness of such subjective experiencing cannot ever be completely revealed. We can approach the meaning of a given seizure of performance anxiety and even recognize its facets, but in the last analysis it defies our complete understanding and resists a definitive exegesis. From the outside, to be sure, we may be able to comprehend correlations of meaning by learning to imagine and understand an individual's stage sets, scenes, and piece. The inner meaning of all this, however, will always be richer and more complex than can be experienced from that vantage-point. Performance anxiety is imbedded in an individual's environment and life story and thus can be understood only from these perspectives. This kind of understanding may represent a limitation, but it is also an enrichment. Therefore, enlightenment will always require a voyage of discovery into human beings' manifold inner landscapes.

Four Typical Ways We React under Stress

Every afflicted person knows best what he means by performance anxiety and how his own performance anxiety feels to him. For the sake of a better orientation, I would like to confine myself to four typical

manifestations of performance anxiety which appear in more or less concentrated form, singly or combined, to each one of us.

a) Bodily Reactions

Performance anxiety is first of all a bodily experience. This experience can utter itself primarily in the cardial area through irregular, fast, or strong heartbeats; in the vascular system through paleness or blushing; in the muscular domain through trembling, cramps, or weak knees; in the respiratory realm by accelerated breathing or a feeling of tightness; and gastrointestinally through stomach pains, gas, diarrhea, belching, a feeling of a lump in the throat, or vomiting. As a reaction of the vegetative nervous system, excessive perspiring, a dilation of the pupils of the eyes, or bladder pressure may occur; and as a reaction of the central nervous system we can experience headaches, fluttering of the eyes, feelings of light-headedness, or fainting.

b) Cognitive Reactions

We cannot concentrate any more, and our memory leaves us in the lurch. We forget details or even important points of orientation. We are confused, even to a total incapacity for thinking, we are broody and anxious, and our thoughts revolve around danger, threats, possible defeats, or catastrophes.

c) Emotional Reactions

We feel ourselves to be in a state of heightened tension, easily irritable, and depressed. Feelings of oppression and anguish appear, coupled with that of not being up to the situation or of being overwhelmed by it. A feeling of helplessness or shame can take over. Panic or loss of control can ensue, reviving old childhood feelings.

d) Behavioral Reactions

We have difficulty falling asleep, and we often awaken during the night or much too early in the morning. Our appetite fails us, or else we eat compulsively, so as to combat the unrest and the fear. We avoid certain situations, because everything is too much for us; or we become hectic and hyperactive, or paralyzed and permanently exhausted.

Even though there are certain similarities between people, there are nevertheless many landscapes hidden behind the mask of performance anxiety. Now the question arises: why does one person react with trembling and another with heavy perspiration, while a third is as if paralyzed? Moreover, it is striking how one's specific stage fright generally attacks one's special activity. Take musicians, for example. Wind-instrument players get a dry mouth, so that their embouchure and sound production are affected. Pianists complain about cold, clammy hands and are afraid of slipping off the keys. Organists are afraid of weak knees, which hamper their pedalling ability; and string players are terrified when their bow arm trembles. In addition, let us think about speaking in public, which is said at the moment to be a principal area for performance anxiety in the United States. How is it that as speakers we happen to get a quivering voice or a lump in the throat, in other words, precisely that which does us the least good?

Vulnerability for Performance Anxiety

The more specialized, stylized, and restricted our approach is to an area of competence or dexterity, the more vulnerable we become precisely in that place

where we define ourselves through our activity.

Our susceptibility to specific individual stage-fright reactions definitely corresponds to our vulnerability. It seems to be first and foremost the artistic and athletic professions—those which do not belong to the basic, existentially necessary ones such as baker, brick-layer, farmer, or doctor—that are particularly vulnerable. They are given over to the essence of the illusory, the element of not being absolutely indispensable for life. Add to this the fact that in these professions the body or the voice has been specialized, perfected, and stylized through rigorous training and is employed in a manner which goes far and above what is necessary for mere daily survival. The more specialized we are in our particular area of competence and the more restrictively, narrowly, or in a stylized way we define ourselves—for example, as the opera singer or the parachutist—the more vulnerable we become precisely in those areas crucial to our ability. Unfortunately, then, it is just those zones on which we have staked our life effort that provide our vulnerability with its most tempting targets. We need only to think of the difference between gypsy musicians and classical violinists. Whereas with the latter we often notice the strain of hard practice, it is a pleasure to see how instinctively a gypsy musician manages his instrument, trusting that he will be able to become one with his listeners.

Performance anxiety, then, is intimately associated with a narrowly defined identification of our capabilities and activities in which patterns of movement have become stereotyped, together with a specialization and a stylizing of certain functions of our bodies. The narrower the patterns through which we define ourselves, the more vulnerable we become, and vice versa: the wider these patterns are

delineated—e. g., choir member, housewife, child, single—
the smaller the target we offer.

Archaic Reactions to Performance Anxiety

**The phylogenetic programs active in our
behavior patterns are first of all biologically sensible
ones. However, they can also lead to dysfunctioning,
since they are often triggered without regard for the
changed circumstances.**

Today we know that in our nervous system, behavior
patterns are embedded which derive from our phylogenetic
past. The further perspective of the evolutionary approach
leads us, in connection with our subject of performance
anxiety, to a deeper understanding of individual and social
dysfunctioning. Anxiety is not bred in a vacuum. It is the
product of a re-shaping, refinement, and sharpening of
elements pre-existing in the realm of animal communities. If
performance anxiety produces attacks of diarrhea or
vomiting, these symptoms are merely a new version of the
reaction of our ancestors, who in the face of danger used to
empty their stomachs so as to be able to save their lives, all
the lighter, when fleeing from predators. It is true that we
have put a great distance between ourselves and the direct
signals of nature. Our purely reflective reactions to certain
events can now be activated by the symbolic meanings we
attach to these events. Nonetheless, we still possess archaic
reflexes, and these can be activated by performance anxiety
in particular.

Three "fossils" play a special role here: flight ("Let's
get out of here"), attack ("Rout the enemy", "Hit him hard"),
and defeat or helplessness ("Duck down and keep quiet until

the coast is clear"). If we survey the animal realm, we will also see the same reactions familiar to us in situations of danger: heartbeat acceleration, muscular tension, helplessness, apathy. The only difference is that an animal reacts in a stereotyped manner according to the behavior patterns of its species, whereas a human being has various possibilities open to him. Human reactions depend largely on the extent of one's personal involvement: that is, how one perceives and rates a situation. In this connection, the social perceptions we have trained and internalized in our primary groups play a fundamental role.

The phylogenetic programs which are still active in our behavior patterns are first of all biologically sensible ones, because they enable us to react with alertness, avoidance, or defense, thus contributing to our organism's balance. However, they can also lead to dysfunctioning, since they often are triggered off without regard for the changed circumstances. Thus it happens that we feel blind rage when someone takes the right of way from us, even though we are not in a hurry; or we become afraid of something, even though the danger perhaps lies in the future; or we are nearly paralyzed in the face of an impending performance, even though nothing but good will is offered to us. To understand such behavior, we will have to look more closely at how such alarm reactions arise.

Performance Anxiety as an Alarm Signal from the Brain

Situations of stress mobilize reaction patterns from the older areas of our brain. Social fears prevent the natural functioning of alarm reactions. Hyperactivity is the result.

57

"Imagine that you are just about to make an important public appearance... Observe what is going on in your body now, how you react to the event..."

The first reaction which you probably notice is a change in your pattern of breathing. Your body is also tensed, you begin to perspire more profusely, your hands begin to tremble imperceptibly, at the same time you cannot think clearly any more, you are confused. As a *homo sapiens* who is used to comport yourself politely and in keeping with the norms of society, you may not use claws or eye-teeth any more, but your body would be ready fight or flight if necessary. What in detail has transpired?

We perceive the signal, "go onstage", via our sensory organs, which lead it on to the brain. There the signal is led by a kind of relay station in the thalamus, which is considered to be the gateway to consciousness, on to the neocortex, the place of conscious perception and thinking. Here the sensory impressions are assembled to form concepts and images, which are relayed on to the limbic system. There an evaluation of the situation takes place— threat, danger, fear—together with the selection of a suitable pattern of behavior, which can be either acquired or hereditary. By way of the hypothalamus, which lies in the middle of the brain and steers all the vegetative processes, and the pituitary gland, which controls the body's hormone production, our body is prepared for the danger by an electrochemical process triggered by a reaction of the sympathetic nervous system. The activity of the sympathetic nervous system—an arm of the autonomous nervous system —aims at direct, immediate action. Under its influence, when the siren of alarm or defense is sounded, blood is pumped into the deeper regions of our muscles, resulting in a change in our hormone level. Adrenaline and noradrenaline are released, effecting a rise in our blood pressure; our pulse rate is also accelerated and our breathing quickened. Our body is thus trimmed to defense within fractions of a second. After the "fight or flight" reaction has been carried out and the mobilized energy consumed, a relaxation reaction sets in (steered by the parasympathetic nervous system).

Stress situations have the tendency to mobilize reaction patterns from the older parts of our brain. The disadvantage of these processes is that disturbances or false alarms are possible, because our neocortex—the younger part of our brain, with which we think, judge, and speak—is often countermanded by the strong signals coming from the limbic system, and to such an extent that the neocortex does not function any more as it should.

In reality, we are no longer threatened by predators which we must fight or from which we must flee, but today—in a society obligating its members to success and the pursuit of happiness—we rather tend to feel threatened when in danger of making ourselves ridiculous or of failing. Our greatest fear, though, is that of being abandoned or rejected. Unfortunately, in such situations many people ignore or disregard their alarm signals, treat them as something irksome or abnormal, and thereby lose the ability to understand their meaning. They talk about lack of sleep, when it is actually fear which comes in the night and robs them of their rest; or they call it fatigue, when they would rather hide or run away. When all the possible explanations are exhausted, the chief offender always remains: the weather. The more we belittle and deny those bodily signals indicating heightened arousal, the more tenacious they will become, the clearer their language: dilated pupils, tightened jaw even to the point of nocturnal gnawing, neck tension, shallow breathing, raised shoulders, and a generally tense posture.

Such alarm signals, then, were originally a biologically correct reaction to dangers and threats, combined with the activation of defense and protective reactions. This picture is questioned when we think of the internal sources of threat coming from images and fantasies and expressed in the painful disturbances of performance anxiety. For an observer, the behavior of a person so afflicted will probably appear exaggerated and unsuitable, but for the sufferer it seems as though the older parts of his brain still continue to urge him to fight or flight, even though in reality such a reaction may not be possible or even necessary.

Fear and performance anxiety comport themselves within a spectrum both of adapted processes completely in keeping with the overcoming of challenges, and unadapted processes which rather diminish the possibilities of such overcoming. Why are we as human beings so susceptible to such processes, more than any other species? After all, the coexistence of the three parts of our brain, originating at successive periods during our phylogenetic development, does provide for alternative reactions, and these do not necessarily need to be disharmonic ones. A proof of this fact is the existence of other cultures, different from ours, which do not suffer from the psychosomatic reactions plaguing us. We will therefore have to go back a step to answer the question.

Modern-day human beings are the result of a self-domestication process which has lasted for 60,000 to 100,000 years. The social adaptations characteristic of all warm-blooded animals were adequate for the early hunters and collectors, but a drastic change in environment took place with the development of agrarian and cattle-breeding society. Population density, crowding, and food resources increased dramatically; but infections also became common, because mankind was not biologically prepared for such developments. The process of natural selection certainly benefitted those individuals who felt at ease in the group, but it also left us with certain other ones who were not so well-adapted, those to whom the density of crowded modern life poses emotional problems. Bodily and psychic damage is the result of these stress reactions due to crowding; for in many of us—the less adapted ones—patterns of behavior still survive which are more characteristic of the archaic reactions of hunters and collectors living in small groups.[19] Seen from this perspective, our modern life is a revolution, a violation of the laws of distance, a total upset, a giant tilt. Animals still have this instinct, they keep their distance, and they would rather go hungry than to give up that certain distance separating them from their neighbors. We on the other hand have grown accustomed to accept unquestioningly the violation of the old distances, those which felt wholesome, as well as the establishment of disastrous new measurements. We would not even admit to suffering from too much closeness. Instead, we accept artificial distances—anonymity, so much glorified and vilified—so that what is near becomes moved far away from us and becomes strange. We allow ourselves to become overwhelmed by what is faraway, strange, and thus fear-inspiring, without realizing that one feeling produces the other. Forced to live in such crowded conditions, we have no other choice than to pretend that we don't know each other. We only feign the natural situation, the one corresponding to our real needs.

Despite the universal availability of psychological knowledge, by storming the barricades of distance and faced with a corresponding spreading of social fears far and wide, our society has erected other barriers and taboos hindersome to the natural functioning of alarm reactions. Since the "steam" thus generated cannot escape, the hormonal and autonomous alarm reactions remain stored in our bodies without relief. As with animals in a cage, our muscles remain tensed; we seem to be plugged into an electrical current, producing symptoms corresponding to never-waning arousal. Chronic hyperactivity of this kind can damage our inner organs, preparing the way for psychosomatic illnesses. Our alarm reactions will become problematic if we do not pay enough attention to them or give them their necessary expression, thus boycotting by ourselves their urgently needed release. The meaning of all this is that we must learn again to make a place for insecurity and fear, as well as for suitable feelings of safety and protection. This is the language—instead of rational control—that the older parts of our brain understand.

Attitudes Specific to Performance Anxiety

Revealing aids to understanding are provided by the treasure chest of popular sayings and by the study of psychosomatic medicine.

Our alarm reactions in performance situations may give us hints that performance anxiety is raising its head, but they do not explain its specific forms of expression. It would seem that everything is taken literally by the bodily and perceptive processes expressed through the various reactions characteristic of performance anxiety. Performance anxiety overcomes us, whether our anxieties or expectations are real or only imagined. How does it happen, then, that some people react by feeling ill at the stomach or in their intestines, others with circulatory disturbances, and still others with binge eating? For what reasons do particular symptoms accompany specific situations? A comprehensive model which would answer these questions does not yet exist. To be sure, a number of studies are available, containing impressive series of statistics and measurements dealing mainly with athletes and musicians, but a satisfactory theory is still lacking. Manifest aids to true understanding, however, are provided by the veritable treasure chest of popular sayings—the language of our daily lives—and by the study of psychosomatics.

There are numerous turns of phrase typical of situations involving performance anxiety. In them, the reciprocity between feelings, situations, and bodily reactions becomes understandable:

It took my breath away.

I was speechless.

It grabs me at the throat.

My mouth went dry.

I've got cold feet.

I did it in my pants.

I have a certain feeling at the back of my neck, at the pit of my stomach.

My stomach did flip-flops.

Keep a stiff upper lip.

I was scared stiff, scared s—less.

I really stuck out my neck.

Keep your chin up!

That just makes me sick.

Someone who can say that he "did it in his pants" is much closer to his real personality than if he were to have used the Latin word "diarrhea". Feelings and bodily happenings are inseparably intertwined, creating a connotation of meaning that points in the direction of what we are missing or what we need. Somebody who says before going onstage that he has cold feet, for example, is capable of hinting at the fact that he feels himself to be overburdened. Our body gives us the signals. If we don't ignore them, we can discover personal insight and hidden meaning. These in turn can show us not only what we are missing, but also what can help us.

Conflicts Specific to Performance Anxiety

Every person has his "fear organ", the one to which his performance anxiety attaches itself. Our inner posture and the extent of our personal involvement determine our bodily reactions to stress situations.

Simplified, one could say that there are two basic patterns of reaction to performance anxiety. There are persons reacting primarily with feelings of aggressivity, competition, and defiance, feelings mainly associated with reactions of the sympathetic nervous system. Others react mainly with needs of retreat, defense, and helplessness, feelings generally having to do with reactions of the parasympathetic nervous system.[20] It has been revealing for me to learn that when the cry to go onstage is uttered, men tend more to reactions of the sympathetic and women more to those of the parasympathetic nervous system. "Sympathetic" persons react with cold sweat, dilation of the pupils, trembling hands, quickened breathing and/or headaches, whereas "parasympathetic" persons do not wish to be spoken to and rather tend towards tiredness, depression, exhaustion, constipation, and/or stomach disorders.

Decisive for our bodily reactions to public stress situations are our inner posture and the extent of personal involvement which we show in the face of a given situation. How we evaluate and cope with the situation is thus the issue. Our bodily reactions take our inner posture literally, representing it directly with the language of our organs. Our bodies select those organs which are at one with our feelings about the situation. Said in another way: from the language of our organs we derive meaningful and decipherable answers to perceived stress situations. Feelings and postures have their own corporeal companions, a constellation which derives from the vegetative nervous system. The nervous system, then, is more than just a receiver of stimuli; it also regulates an individual's relationship to his group. What we designate as social pressure or necessity for adaptation is perceived by the individual as an emotional sensation, and this is activated by neurophysiological processes. For this reason, Jonas describes the nervous system as a mediator between the individual and his group.[21]

In my numerous discussions of performance anxiety I have been able to collect a large number of characteristic symptoms making clear the close connection between one's personal attitude to an event and the respective accompanying bodily processes. Here I would like to present a list of the most frequently occurring reactions, in their relation to specific inner postures.

Cold, clammy hands occur frequently when a person is constrained to perform a given action but is uncertain, because he is not properly prepared or does not know exactly what is to be done. Cold hands have to do with retreat, and with the fear of letting go, trusting, and opening oneself up ("Don't you dare touch me"). Extremely cold hands can also have to do with aggressive impulses ("I would just love to flail away"). They are the result of a narrowing of the blood vessels, which produces a loss of warmth. For gross motor skills such a loss of warmth may be desirable, but for fine motor activities it is rather a hindrance.

Diarrhea often has to do with the wish to get out of an unpleasant situation as soon as possible. One would like to free oneself from a given situation and get it over with ("Oh, if this concert could only be over already"). The opposite syndrome, **constipation**, tends to arise when one is determined to last a given situation out and stick to it ("No matter how the outcome is, I won't give up").

Muscular tensions receive their meaning when they are viewed from the aspect of a defensive gesture. If one is expecting an imaginary blow, then one tenses the muscles of one's head, chest, and abdomen—a protective reaction to minimize the danger of being hurt ("It is as if my hands were tied"). Those neck pains that often turn up in a given situation when a person is embarrassed also belong to this category. As an archaic remnant of a gesture of submission, we bow our heads when we are ashamed or humiliated; but our brain, making a decision, releases the countermanding order to hold the head high. Our neck muscles thus receive contradictory commands, tighten, and hurt ("Keep your chin up!").

These examples clarify the ways in which specific symptoms can be understood as the symbolic language of our bodies. Feelings, postures, and bodily reactions always take place simultaneously and are rooted within the inner milieu of our organism. Of course, it is not always possible to make an unequivocal attribution, but there are at least certain characteristic patterns and observations giving us important points of departure for coping with performance anxiety. Fundamentally, we know that those afflicted must learn to take a closer look at the "no" which they have expressed up till now through their symptoms, in order to recognize the connection between their body and their feelings, so that their blocked movement can be discovered and set free.

4

Psychological Aspects of Performance Anxiety

Through performance anxiety, the discrepancy between demands and our possibilities of overcoming them announces itself.

Performance anxiety is not only an integral part of our evolutionary heritage, triggered by certain alarm devices within our bodies associated with survival. It is also the specific expression of our fear of certain situations which we perceive as threatening to our personal integrity. Why does it not break out for every person with the same intensity, we ask, and why do some persons in performance situations suspect dangers which for others are non-existent? Besides the outer causes, then, there must also be some inner ones. These are to be sought in the structure of an individual's personality.

The general function of performance anxiety seems to lie therein, that any discrepancy existing between real or expected demands made on us by particular public situations and our possibilities of overcoming them, based on self-preservation, is immediately announced. On the one hand, the discrepancy can lie in our inability of controlling possible threats or expectations coming from our environment. On the other hand it can have to do with possible threats to our personal integrity being expected as a loss of self-control. In both cases, performance anxiety is a presentiment erecting a barricade against the uncertainty of the future. In the last analysis, it is connected with our deeper inner knowledge as to being abandoned to all the doubts, uncertainties, imponderabilities, ... in short: the vicissitudes of life.

Sometimes we meet up with people who in daily circumstances seem to be able to state their case well enough, but when they have to give a speech suddenly become panic-stricken, whereas in the same situation people who are otherwise nervous develop an admirable calmness. Sometimes even those people who, at the lectern, exude self-confidence in exemplary fashion can become terrified when asked to play the piano at a friend's house. These examples show that the same situation can have different meanings for different people, meanings which are dependent on a given individual's personal involvement.

If we wish to inquire after the common factor of various situations involving performance anxiety, then we must differentiate between situations of a strongly social character, such as speeches at banquets or concerts, and other situations in which the audience plays only a secondary role, such as parachute jumping or riflery. Furthermore, there are situations in which self-confidence is required and we are exposed to the judgment of others and evaluated. The reference to the future is a distinguishing feature of such situations. An essential factor is whether a given situation is perceived to have an important influence on our destiny, such as a job application or a test, or is less important for our future, such as a house concert or a football game among friends. Particularly predestined for performance anxiety are situations representing a danger to our feeling of self-worth, the loss of benevolent attention from people serving as important role models, or the loss of material goods.

Expectations

Expectations which we phantasize as coming from outside can strike back at us as an independent, sometimes even monstrous force and turn into expectations of our own; and these can be even more perfectionistic than the ones we meet with from outside.

To a certain degree, performance anxiety is always associated with an outer judge; that is, with persons or groups sending expectations our way. These persons can be parents, teachers, colleagues, or a more or less large audience. Sometimes we know by ourselves what others expect of us, but usually we presume or phantasize, thereby feeling ourselves to be under pressure or having to prove something. We attribute to others not only expectations, but also a series of roles involving judgment or prejudice: in particular, the role of the critic, the punisher, the judge, or the censor. Expectations which we phantasize as coming from outside can strike back at us as an independent, sometimes even monstrous force and turn into expectations of our own; and these can be much stricter and even more perfectionistic than the ones we meet with from outside. A wrong word or a sour note, one often not even noticed by our listeners, can become inflated to catastrophic proportions, because our own grandiose expectations are so unrealistic and unmerciful. Basically, these high expectations derive from our wanting to do our best.

Precisely for this reason we try to ferret out anything that can be rated as bad or as a mistake. We want to show how good we are and that we have something to offer which is worth being seen or heard and which can fulfil real or imagined expectations. If we are good, we are the winner; if we fail, then we are on the losing side and fall into discredit. It is usually just before performances, sometimes even days ahead, that these fears of expectations culminate; but they usually ebb away quickly once a performance is over. As opposed to diffuse anxieties, we are dealing here with short-lived fears centered around a particular event, fears in which, next to the obvious obstructing influences, a kind of respect for our society's ideals and values is also expressed.

During the course of our development, expectations directed at us by our nearest role models become internalized; that is, they become a part of our self. There is a direct line of outside expectations, beginning with our fear of our mother's expectations, leading to fear of those of persons of authority, and culminating in the fear of what has been called our "inner eye", the observing eye of our conscience or inner voices.[22] Here, expectations from outside become reflected and amplified by inner ones. These as inner voices consolidate to take on personality traits, replacing the testing, weighing scrutiny or threatening tone of our parents or of those who eventually come to replace them as figures of authority. Although many forms of psychotherapy tend to take the negative side of these inner voices as their point of departure, such as the "superego" (Freud) or the "shadows" (Jung), we also internalize our parents' good, caring aspects. However, it is usually the critical, accusing voices which we notice, since they inhibit and constrict us.

With performance anxiety, these inner testers and referees center themselves most of all around a fundamental

71

trio: the inner judge, the doubter, and the timid soul. Interestingly enough, these three inner voices represent exactly the opposite qualities of those expected in performances, namely, self-esteem, conviction, and courage—our inner friends. Although the qualities represented by all these inner parties may seem to be contradictory, they nevertheless are dependent on each other and presuppose one other. How shall I know what self-esteem is, if I have never experienced self-judgment? Another comparison: How can I know what hunger is, if I have never experienced satiety? Only when I am familiar with both sides of the coin can I find my own personal share. Two principles apply here: the principle of polarity, Gestalt therapy speaking of "top dog" and "underdog"; and the principle of integration, a reconciliation of both sides.

If we now look at performance anxiety once again from this perspective, the following happens: the closer our public appearance comes, the more we begin to doubt in our capability of living up to certain expectations, either imposed by ourselves or coming from outside. We place first our capabilities and possibilities, then ourselves in doubt, even condemning ourselves because of this. The entire gauntlet of our inner judges raises its index finger and shouts down the voices of our inner defenders with whom they originally sought contact, so that the latter are completely overheard and cannot get a word in edgewise.[23] No dialogue, and thus no reconciliation, can take place—instead, we are trembling and have leaden feet.

Performance Anxiety Has Many Faces

An integrative approach tends to come closest to the complex demands of a treatment of performance

Performance anxiety shows itself at the line of demarcation between intended self-exposure—which depending on one's demands is situated between wanting to be good, better, or ideal—and realizing the possibility of not attaining the desired result in front of witnesses. It anticipates the possible consequences of our self-chosen showing-off. However, it is the very quality of anxious awaiting found in such situations that practically begs stage fright to break out, requiring us to redirect our attention inwards, away from the situation or task at hand. Worried selfish thoughts—also called the "worry factor" in American research on test anxiety—lead to heightened self-centeredness, bringing on that very condition we were trying to avoid.[24] If we doubt being able to "make it", a reduction in our performance efficiency is bound to be the result. If we fear the scoffers' laughter, we will curtail our own spontaneity. The fear of failure creates failure! In truth, there is a whole army of people who have failed in school whose unsuccessfulness was due not to their insufficient intelligence, but to their fear of failure. Of course, we cannot deny that there are also teachers whose pedagogical ability is not exactly conducive to a reduction in their pupils' fears of failure. However, as a rule it is parents' high expectations of accomplishments which trigger off their children's fear of failure, often before school has even begun. Already in the first years of life, too strict toilet training, principles of behavior, or aptitude expectations can lead to the fear of failure. Many children very early get the message: "You are only worth something when you achieve something". Many parents will have nothing to do with the idea that it was they who set their child's exaggerated anxieties in motion—since unconscious motives connected with their own repressed fears of failure are often hidden behind their demands.

A possible explanation for performance anxiety could theoretically lie in the fact that our fear of failure is hereditary, that there are simply persons more or less predisposed to fear. If this hypothesis were to be true, then we wouldn't have any chance of getting rid of our anxiety. Another factor speaking against this hypothesis is that during the course of our lives we can actually lose our fear of certain situations, for example, fear of the water, fear of school, etc. The behavioristic approach, which is most prevalent in the United States, answers this question with the basic statement that since performance anxiety represents acquired behavior, conditioned through repetition, by the same token it can also be un-learned. The cognitive models and the scholars of so-called attribution theory go a step further: they assume that fear only arises when one's coping strategies are not sufficient for a given situation.[25] Incapability of coping with a given situation is experienced as fear-inspiring. These scholars assume that human beings attribute their helplessness to themselves, thereby developing a fearful avoidance pattern in order to protect their feeling of self-worth.

Even though these models offer plausible explanations for how stage fright originates, the question still remains: why doesn't performance anxiety stop by itself when we see time and again that it was not justified? According to theories of learning and behavior, it ought to become forgotten if we learn repeatedly that there is no reason for it.

The ways human beings express fears are so sophisticated and complex that an exclusively cognitive approach cannot furnish a perfect solution to the specific problem of performance anxiety. With this affliction, symptoms arise on several levels; we are thus dealing with a complex pattern of reactions. With some individuals, it may indeed be acquired fears, with others, the repression of experiences traumatic to their feeling of self-worth, and with a third group, organic overreactions, which come into play. Usually several factors strengthen each other reciprocally.

Performance anxiety, then, has many faces, and this insight also has its consequences for treatment. Whereas it used to be a debatable question as to whether, basically, the methods of psychoanalysis, counselling, behavior therapy, or general arousal suppression should be applied, today multidimensional, integrative models of treatment seem to be most promising. That these models offer some hope of success is mainly because their approach is not only centered on the symptoms, but is also capable of keeping an eye on the entire person at the same time, with all his individual ways of expression. My experience in my own practice has shown that an integrative procedure best approaches the complex demands required by a treatment of performance anxiety. With such an approach not only reparative, calming processes are activated, but also beneficial ones which cause our imagination and sensitivity to unfold. Before treating these manifold processes, I would like to delve still deeper into the spiritual background of performance anxiety and concentrate on a key term: our feeling of self-worth.

Evaluation and the Feeling of Self-Worth

Our fear of exposure results from the reciprocal action between how we are evaluated from outside, earlier evaluations, and the esteem in which we hold ourselves.

Here we arrive at the core of what makes up our performance anxiety: the fear of exposure, of losing face in such a way that quite embarrassingly, what and who we are is revealed. Since such exposure normally affects persons who enjoy placing themselves in the limelight, it hits them still harder, for it illuminates pitilessly the way in which they overestimated their own capacities. If one overestimates oneself and is shown up, one's feeling of self-worth shrinks, giving way to the shame of failure or rejection. An important conflict inherent in the spectrum of performance anxiety is thus between one's power ploy, directed outwards or inwards, and the realization of one's own weakness, especially in front of an observing public. Most of all we fear others' laughter, for it was we who chose to step into the limelight in the first place, and thus we have only ourselves to blame.

In essence, performance anxiety has to do with our feeling of self-worth. It is always is related to the trio of value, power, and failure, and thus to extremely vulnerable aspects of our self. The deeper these conflicts are, the more they affect our feeling of self-worth, and the more massively fears are released and protective measures become necessary. The content of such conflicts is grouped around various themes: "I am meaningless and cannot be worth anything to anyone", "I am weak, helpless, and a failure in competitive situations", "I am not at all perfect, but rather puny and insignificant", or "I am afraid of making myself look ridiculous".

As far as these typical statements are concerned, the question is: who is the one doing the rating? When I ask my clients this question, I always find three channels of rating: the others (audience, group, superiors), earlier role models, and oneself. Our fear of exposure thus results from the reciprocal action between how we are evaluated from outside, earlier evaluations, and the esteem in which we hold ourselves. Said in another way: it is a matter of the reciprocity between what is expected, how we want to be seen, and how we perceive ourselves. A determining factor is public discovery. All eyes seem to be focussed on us, we yearn only for the advantage of disappearing: we would rather vanish into the ground. We wish ourselves far away from the curse of our judges or simply of those who embarrass us by their presence.

The other question is: if there is going to be an evaluation, what are the criteria? Do they have some relation to reality, or are they distorted, irrational expectations, such as: "I have to be loved and accepted by everyone", "I shall always be efficient and successful", or "I will only be respected if my performance is perfect"? As we can see, the character of these statements is heavily influenced by the ideal picture we make of ourselves, seeing ourselves the way we would like to be. If it was originally parental figures who determined their desired picture of us, in that they idealized us and we them, in the course of our development these ideals gradually become a guiding picture of our own behavior, of our own inner expectations. The more unrealistic parents' expectations are—not only the outer, articulated ones, but also and especially the unspoken ones—and the more they deny the child's emotional world, the greater will be the discrepancy between the "ideal child" and the "real child". Such internalized expectations often attach themselves to other persons, to our superiors, or to our audience, via the typical self-conscious question: "What are they thinking about me?"

Idealizations can spurn us on to peak performances. However, they can also inhibit us if parents overburden their child with idealized expectations, thereby preparing the terrain for repeated disappointments and fear of belittlement. The larger the discrepancy between the way we would like to be and our perception of how and what we really are, all the more will we fear exposure and with it, performance anxiety itself.

The Star Complex

Pitiless self-deprecation as well as its opposite, excessive narcissism, are rooted in our own delusions of grandeur.

Conflicts related to our ideal picture of ourselves and our "grand self" are recognizable in that they possess a global character.[26] This derives from the fact that they arose at a time during development when the original reciprocal influencing was characterized by global feelings, wishes, and pictures, a time in which the infant was the idol of his parents' eye. According to Kohut, one's "grandiose self" presents itself as a fixation at an archaic stage of the self, one in which a child experiences itself as though, magically, it could dominate the world. This is a period of illusions of unlimited omnipotence and of pride at the acquisition of grandiose capabilities.[27] Normally, this rapture does not last long. A child, when it begins to mature, gets in a position where it is able to recognize and accept its limitations, so that its "grandiose self" changes into a more or less realistic feeling of self-worth. However, when this integration becomes disturbed, then the fertile soil becomes prepared for illusions of grandeur and greed for admiration, and in their absence, for the sheer bottomless feeling of being totally worthless.

To a certain degree, such illusions are slumbering to a certain degree in nearly every human being. However, they are supported by a relatively stable feeling of the ego and lead to only minimal fluctuations of one's feelings of self-worth. How much more dangerous and seductive, then, is the plague of such phantasies of grandeur that we meet in the so-called star complex, devolving daily before our eyes in the world of opera, football, the theater, pop-music culture, and the film world! As long as these "stars" or "favorites" are courted and praised to the skies by our own projected dreams and wishes, their audiences' shining eyes are enough for them. If this confirmation should be absent, however, even the most illustrious of them can plummet from heaven, as shown by the biographies of countless stars who once were the hope of entire nations.

Performance anxiety is nourished by the Grandiose Self in the form of intense claims on perfection and overproduction. In the most favorable cases, these can serve as pacemakers for record performances. In unfavorable ones, through their exaggerated demands, they can actually frustrate the attainment of reachable goals. The great things expected of the Grandiose Self, knowing no boundaries, exert an inhibiting influence precisely in the areas of self-exposure, because we are thus led to persecute every self-revelation and every self-expression with pitiless criticism. Such merciless self-deprecation, as well as its exact opposite—the self-overestimation of many people who are oriented towards achievement, who believe that through their activity for others they have a right to their affection— are rooted in their own feelings of grandeur. We only need to look behind the scenes just before a performance in order to see the drama of grandiosity and self-devaluation devolving at an accelerated pace. We would almost like to push a given actor onto the stage, because he is paralyzed by fear as if his life were at stake. Viewed symbolically, his life really is at stake; since the more pronounced his identification with the Grandiose Self is and the greater his necessity of confirmation from outside, all the greater is the danger of loss of self and the fear behind it of deprivation of love.

Such phantasies of grandeur tend to be embarrassing to many persons who place themselves in the limelight. First it is their feeling of embarrassment at becoming unmasked, having had their phantasies exposed, and being seen as immodest, that plays a role. If this feeling is accompanied by a strong disposal towards rivalry, then such persons' sensitivity to their own deficiencies increases boundlessly. The way they deal with applause and admiration finally becomes a tightrope walk between their shame and their underlying greed for admiration and grandeur. On the one hand they are afraid of admiration, but on the other they are constantly looking for it and are deeply offended when the awaited echo fails to appear.

We all are in need of an echo, of resonance. It only becomes dangerous for us when this need degenerates into dependence. For the development of a healthy feeling of self-worth, therefore, it is necessary for a child's persons of reference to enter sensitively into his wishes and be attuned to them. Our feelings of self-worth depend decisively on the experienced evaluations and devaluations with which we are confronted from early childhood. Therefore, the origin and early development in our life history of our particular type of feeling of self-worth shall be more closely illuminated below.

Old and New Scenes

If devaluing, belittling scenes and atmospheres become impressed on our consciousness early on, then

the stage is set for a detrimental development of our feeling of self-worth and for conflicts in the area of showing and expressing ourselves.

The "mirror" of the eyes and faces of loving persons of reference forms the foundation of our faculty of conquering a place in life in keeping with our personality, of showing ourselves or being seen, of impressing or fascinating others or revealing ourselves through our self-expression, without exaggerated inhibitions.[28] The need to be seen in the shining eyes of an audience, to fascinate, or to charm, has its origins on this early stage set. It is certainly understandable that there is a big difference as to whether I have learned that I have elbow-room and am allowed to express myself in the presence of others, or if my first faltering steps at self-expression were met by cold gazes, indifference, or controlling infringements. Said in another way: if at an early age scenes and atmospheres of belittlement become impressed on our consciousness, then the stage is set for a detrimental development of our feeling of self-worth and our image of it, as well as for future conflicts and vulnerabilities in the areas of perception and being perceived, of showing and expressing ourselves. Abysses will open up between the way in which we perceive ourselves and what others expect of us, or between the way we are and would like to be. Since expectations and reality do not seem to correspond, we will begin to mistrust our own perceptions and self-expression. Victory and defeat, power and impotence, love and unlovedness, worth and unimportance—all these scenes are acted out by parents and child on the early stage set of perception and expression. All the various scenes of the dialogue of glances, the musical dialogue of voices, and the rhythm of reciprocal expression sink into the background of consciousness, and from that vantage-point they continue to have an effect on the present. If in the present a similar scene should arise, then old scenes will become revived on the new stage, thus influencing the here and now. Our insight into the connection between past scenes with their atmospheres, and new scenes they bring to the fore, creates what we call our "own story", with the continuity and security of behavior belonging to it. However, if we are not conscious of the effect of old patterns, or if we must constantly repeat old scenes and scenarios even though the present calls for new solutions, then our story will also be endangered by a one-sided fixation on these old solutions.

With performance anxiety, not only current expectations and fears are condensed, but also past atmospheres and scenes become actualized along with them, flowing more or less consciously or unconsciously into the situation of the here and now. This dimension in time implies that every scene of performance anxiety may be new, but never completely so. We stage not only scenes, but also their form and shape. These become compressed into particular structures which in their turn become internalized.[29] Such structures can subsequently turn up in the most distinct situations where they can be recognized as similar, for example: "Always the same mistakes", "Once again a typical reaction", "Oh no, not again!" The durable quality of these structures, to be sure, grants them a certain continuity, but—and here is their dark side—it can also result in fixed, crusted-over repetitive patterns which inhibit spontaneous, flexible reactions. In and of themselves, such structures are neither negative nor pathological. They only become so when, rising out of the unconscious, they deterministically influence every new situation, thus cramping our latitude for action and expression or even preventing it entirely.

Panicky, overwhelming performance anxiety allows us to deduce that from within the archives of our body and soul, early atmospheres of fear or belittlement are surfacing; and we become "confluent", that is, inundated by streams of unutterable feelings overwhelming the observing ego. Here our life career—our career of failing or succeeding, a chain of negative or positive experiences leading to a more or less stable identity—plays a decisive role. In the context of our performance anxiety, the story of our belittlements is most significant, for every time we go onstage, we are confronted with inner and outer evaluation. Furthermore, our anxious behavior in the face of performance is not necessarily the result of personal experiences or occurrences. It can also come from our observation of the behavior of persons of reference. For many of us, for example, to see a friend or sibling be repeatedly made a laughing-stock or belittled by a parent or teacher would already suffice for massive anxieties to become mobilized. Such self-identification with others, or empathizing with another's role, can be just as effective and can influence our own behavior just as lastingly as our own personal experience. Therefore, if we wish to speak of fear-releasing devices, we must cast our net of experiences still further: even a witnessed experience can become a trigger to fear!

Not to surrender to the compulsion of old atmospheres, scenes, evaluations, and fears: this is the issue in coping with performance anxiety. In addition, this requires our recognizing the archives of our body and soul where scenes we have experienced and the feelings they evoke have been stored, and understanding their meaning. For severe disturbances of one's feeling of self, a therapist's help will be necessary, since in the treatment of performance anxiety it is not only a matter of understanding oneself, but also of living through old scenes once again and experiencing understanding from another person. New positive experiences and evaluations grow out of situations such as these.

"Emotional Differentiation" Work

The basic attitude of interested curiosity makes it possible for us to step out of involvement and into an committed distance to ourselves.

Anyone wishing to come to terms actively with his performance anxiety will have to work on what I call "emotional differentiation". This means that we learn to distinguish between the many different facets, aspects, or appearances of the emotions involved with stage fright; or to go beyond thinking in terms of black and white, the all-or-nothing approach. It's like dealing with addiction: we have to rediscover and deal with the nuances.

Emotional differentiation, first of all, presupposes our affirmation that the past continues to have an effect on our present activity. We have to be ready to look at what is there and to sensitize ourselves to the phenomenon of performance anxiety. Since every "performance" is specific—that is, we have different reactions at different times and places—the accompanying anxiety has to be perceived and evaluated situationally. Thus it will be possible for us to develop an understanding or a feeling for performance anxiety in a given situation, so that we can begin to grasp what is going on right here and now. Many of those afflicted by performance anxiety are victims of it for the very reason that they repress it and don't want to have a look at it. Searching for the small signs of our affliction is necessary, however, if we are to recognize and understand its various personal patterns, contours, and rituals.

In this connection, there are some helpful questions which we often are able to answer only after the event. "Was there something that came out of another situation into this one?" "Where have I met these feelings before?" "What course do my conversations with myself take before I go onstage?" "Which inner voices can be heard particularly well?" "What does my body express?" These questions offer us the possibility of a deepened self-experience. By listening to our inner monologues or dialogues and to what they have to say, we no longer remain their victim: recognizing them, we can influence them.

Our inner voices, then, are always a mixture of projections of previous experiences, combined with new impressions and experiences. For instance, if we have already heard at an early age that we are industrious, or boring, or whatever, then these evaluations also flow more or less consciously into our present self-evaluation in the form of self-definitions. If we succeed in becoming conscious of these projections and in recognizing them for what they are, then we are no longer at their mercy. We have to do some work on our consciousness and become clear in our minds as to: What is the issue? What are old, obsolete messages? What new alternatives do I have? Which new answers can I give myself? When we pose ourselves these questions, our old messages lose their compulsive force. We can even employ them constructively, ally ourselves with them, or neutralize their destructivity.

This procedure assumes a basic attitude of interested curiosity in the face of what is welling up from within. Such an attitude allows us to step out of involvement or ensnarement and into a committed distance to ourselves. Interested curiosity is not compatible with excluding, splitting off, or self-chastising. It is open for what is coming and tolerant, in the sense of allowing what wishes to show itself to do so. Moreover, interested curiosity is associated with attentiveness towards ourselves. We should hearken intently inwards, instead of repressing and not wanting to admit. Thus instead of fighting against ourselves, we become our own compassionate friends. Matthias Claudius once said that we have to discover for ourselves the master within us. I believe that we can approach this path when we begin to encounter ourselves with committed curiosity. If we can stop splitting our performance anxiety off, denying it, or fighting it, we can become free for new steps on the path of accepting ourselves as we are—but neither better nor worse than that.

5

Coping with Performance Anxiety

If we display the attitude, "Let it come", our performance anxiety will lose its curse.

First of all we have to take as our point of departure the fact that performance anxiety is simply "there". It is neither possible nor desirable to silence it, for it is a valuable companion preparing our body with energy, intensity, tension, and enthusiasm for our performance. To be able to be motivated at all for a performance, a certain quantity of tension is even necessary. Someone who goes onstage de-tensed, that is, completely free of tension, would hardly exude enthusiasm, energy, and intensity—three elements which are absolutely necessary to capture an audience's attention. If we show ourselves to a public, we need a certain energy level. After all, we wish to transmit our involvement, our commitment, and our message so that our effect on the audience is contagious and inspiring. Our audience would feel itself betrayed, or at least not adequately respected, if we were to show ourselves in a too negligent or neutral way.

Therefore, performance anxiety is first and foremost a valuable ally. It gives us the tension we need in order to be involved in the matter we are representing and to awaken involvement in others. Moreover, it protects us, because it provides us with extra energy for carrying our project through from its preparation to the end of the performance. It spurs us on to work, warns us to prepare ourselves well, and delivers us the energy that we need to obtain attention and respect for ourselves. However—and now comes the provocative question—why are these qualities not available just before a performance? Why are these magic moments, in which we feel our "footlight fever" to be a friend, so rare?

Almost everybody has heard of Murphy's or Parkinson's Law. Here is the irony of performance anxiety: the more we try to avoid or ignore it, the greater it becomes. Just when we wish not to be afraid, we are more afraid than ever. Related to this syndrome is the so-called Rosenthal Effect, which enters when we occupy ourselves with possible catastrophes; for the more we think about them, the more magnetically we evoke them. Everything we are imagining is taken literally by our unconscious. If we occupy ourselves with dismal prophecies, we actually activate negative programs in our unconscious which produce exactly what we fear. We become victims of our own self-fulfilling prophecies.

If we admit to ourselves that we have performance anxiety and are permitted to have it, we can interrupt this vicious circle. If we begin to allow it to come out of hiding, to unmask, recognize, and understand it, it loses its curse. Instead of battle or repression, we need to work on reconciliation. The required attitude can be stated succinctly: LET IT COME.

A first step is hearkening to our inner voices. In my practice I use the term "our inner monsters" for the voices tormenting us. The word "monster" allows pictures or ideas to be evoked that give these inner voices their embodiment. Besides, with this choice of words we express the fact that these voices often inflate themselves or attach importance to themselves to such a degree that other, benevolent voices are overheard or even shouted down. In order to take up better contact with our inner monsters, I feel it important that we give them names. In this way, it is easier to address them directly and bargain with them. One thing is important: generalization for the sake of simplification is useful, but the inner monsters are not the same with everyone. They vary in size, tactics, their shadings, and in their behavior.

Our Inner Monsters

Three inner monsters are most responsible for stage fright: the judge, the doubter, and the timid soul.

Everyone knows his own inner monsters, and with each one of us they take on a slightly different form. For some they are very powerful, and for others they only appear in certain restricted areas. Nevertheless, they have many common features making it possible to introduce now the most common monsters associated with performance anxiety. Three monsters are the most responsible for this condition: the inner judge, the doubter, and the timid soul. In this connection I would like to make mention of the inspiring book by Robert Triplett, *Stagefright*.[30] I owe much stimulation concerning my work with inner voices to him; and he is an organist, too.

The Inner Judge
This monster plays a classical role in the drama of performance anxiety. When I let my clients paint this monster, they often represent a stern, ascetic-looking fellow with a raised index finger. Our inner judge can be

recognized by the fact that he always knows what is going to happen: the worst. He is interested in our mistakes, our inexactitudes, and our weaknesses. "Still another lapse!" "What a stupid mistake!" "How can you be this way?" "You can't go in front of people looking like that!" Alert and with a sharp eye, he follows our actions and is lavish with his scorn. His choice of words is not exactly subtle, and it comes mainly from the area of belittlement: "stupid", "dumb", "unbelievable".

Hand in hand with the judge, a related monster often enters: the perfectionist. He, too, wishes for us to perform perfectly. He even gives us hope and stimulation. "If you would only exert yourself a little more!" "That could be still better!" "Did you think of everything?" "You ought to get up still earlier in the morning!" "Pull yourself together!" The perfectionist's vocabulary is controlling, rigid, and absolute. He knows what is to be done and how, and utters himself mostly in a commanding voice: "You ought to", "You must". In my client's pictures he often holds a whip, which helps him to collaborate with the judge. The sweet that he holds in his other hand and with which he wins the judge over, is his reward: a perfect performance.

As long as judge and perfectionist ally themselves for healthy goals of performance improvement and self-discipline, they appear as valuable, helpful companions whom we need in order to develop still further and to exercise self-criticism. However, if their alliance is dedicated to unrealistic, unattainable desires such as "win at any price", "do anything, but do it faster", "either - or", then the foundation is laid for compulsivity, insecurity, and disappointment. If we let the perfectionist get the upper hand, then we come to employ inhuman standards of comparison which deeply undermine our feeling of self-worth. Perfection, when it becomes attached to rigid goals and standards, is first of all inhuman, because we are thus reduced to machines. Second, it is dangerous, because we can become dependent on an illusion that can take on an addictive character if the word is: "Only if I am perfect am I a worthwhile person".

When the perfectionist is at the helm, he activates still another monster within us, the doubter, who questions if we are capable of living up to the standards we set up for ourselves.

The Inner Doubter

This monster expresses himself through skepticism. "Will I make it?" "Isn't that too difficult for me?" "What if...?" His main characteristics are insecurity and uncertainty. The nearer a given event comes, the more active the doubter becomes. "O Lord, only one more day!" "Are you sure you'll be ready?" The doubter appeals to caution and common sense and lives above all in the future. If we allow ourselves to be advised by this voice, still another monster will often appear helpfully on the scene: the coward. At first, the coward seems to belong to our allies, for he recommends: "Just call it all off!" "You just took on too much!" "The others can do it much better anyway!" "How would it be with getting sick?" However, his recommendations are not what we need either, for we want to escape from the doubter with something that gives us a feeling of security.

There is, in fact, another related voice promising us help: the dogmatist. He knows what is right and which path to take. For many of us, his answers and recommendations are accompanied by an inner picture of a guru or a schoolmaster admonishing us: "What you need is more discipline!" "Think positively!" "Concentrate!" "You ought to meditate every day!" The dogmatist's solutions, to be sure, may appear more reasonable than the coward's, but they are not very helpful, since they don't take the doubter's insecurity seriously. His recipes therefore tend to create still more confusion, for who isn't aware of the well-known knot in the brain which arises when somebody orders us to concentrate? The imperative—concentrate!—cancels itself out, for at the moment when such a thought arises, we are already tensed or preoccupied. We thus prevent ourselves from concentrating by concentrating on the fact that we should concentrate... A typical example of this kind of knot occurring during performance is the well-known memory slip. The more we strain ourselves to remember, the worse it becomes. Or when we make a mistake: the more we pull ourselves together to do everything right from then on, the greater the danger that we tense up and become still more knotted up. Knots cannot be undone by orders, increased tension, or exertion, but rather by the opposite: by letting go.[31] Suddenly what has been forgotten pops up, and we find the thread again.

The Timid Soul

This monster reacts to the inner judge and the doubter by retreat. One of my clients depicted her timid soul as a tiny whimpering child, and another expressed him through heart-rending tones on a children's violin. His voice indeed resembles these sounds, and it is precisely because of his helplessness that he is so powerful. The timid soul gives us excuses for our feelings of incapability and passivity. There is surely no more effective way of treading on the spot than by making oneself small and stupid. By such conduct, we can get out of duties and avoid responsibility. Perhaps there is someone out there who could jump in and help? This monster is cunning, because behind his pleading phrases— "I don't know...", "I feel so ill...", "I just can't..."—he has a whole litany of answers ready and waiting: "...because it's too strenuous", "...because the others... ", "...because I'm too untalented (dumb, fearful, etc.)". In addition, he is not completely free of envy, for the others are somehow better anyway. "If I only had the support (time, energy, etc.) that he (she) does...". "If I were only as pretty (handsome) as she (he) is...", etc. Unfortunately, this monster is only wishing for us to remain weak and dependent, to give outer circumstances the blame, and to pull out of the affair.

There is still another ally, one who takes pity on the timid soul: the protector. He always has many good arguments at hand explaining why we cannot live up to our obligations, why we can put something off or get out of it entirely. He protects our timid soul with the cloak of pity : "Treat yourself to some rest first", "First give yourself a square meal", "Forget it, perhaps it will take care of itself", "Probably nobody will notice". This monster has a seductive voice, because he twists things around so that our apparent incapability becomes confirmed and we really and truly do not arrive at what we would have been capable of. If we yield to this siren's voice, it can cast such a spell over us that when suddenly the moment of our appearance, or of when we have to hand something in, has arrived, nobody is there to save us. Now it is too late.

Apparent Maneuvers for Fighting Performance Anxiety

There are helpful strategies, but there are also apparent maneuvers for fighting performance anxiety. When viewed superficially, they often differ from one another only infinitesimally, but the difference in their effectiveness is all the greater.

Helpful strategies call for further development and change. Apparent maneuvers, however, are oriented towards security and the preservation of the status quo. They are not always easily identified and are often hard to grasp, because their more or less sophisticated tactics, viewed from outside, are often not recognizable as such.

A favorite tactic is the "if only" one. "If I only had had more time to prepare this speech", "If only I didn't have so many appointments", "It was not until yesterday that I was able to concentrate on the matter", "If only I hadn't drunk so much last night", "If only I could sleep better", etc. It is so much easier to assign guilt to the circumstances, the pressures of events, or a particular misfortune, than to oneself. The *modus operandi* of this tactic is quite sophisticated, for when we have found excuses, explanations, and justifications, we compel others to spare us, not to expect too much of us, and not to judge us too critically. By excusing ourselves, we anticipate the others' critical judgment, make ourselves unassailable, and can keep face. The unspoken promise transmitted thereby, that of course the next time we will be better prepared, is included at no extra charge. However, this promise is often broken, and we have to look for the next excuse. Such maneuvers are short-lived. First, word gets around that we were ill, etc., once again. Second, with time our listeners become insensitive to our streak of bad luck. Before we know it, we have forfeited their good opinion of us. In a nutshell: if we have neither the time nor the energy to live up to our own expectations, then we had better not accept challenges putting us in the limelight and which only result in our bombarding ourselves and our fellows with excuses.

Another facet of this tactic, which is capable of garnering us not only pity but also the highest admiration, is the argument of unfavorable conditions. However our various excuses may run—from the weather, the time, and the acoustics up to the short period of preparation: it is always the circumstances that prevented us from showing ourselves at our best. How good we'd be now, if we'd only had optimal conditions! Through such explanations we transmit the impression that we would naturally have been capable of much more, if only... With this tactic, then, two goals are achieved: the others give us the handicap of extenuating circumstances and don't expect too much of us, and we create the impression of actually being much better than we were a moment ago. Furthermore, we spare ourselves taking the responsibility for our actions, in that we veil reality from ourselves with the hope of an uncertain future. I know musicians who, after concerts, customarily excuse themselves, and this often just at the moment when I would like to congratulate them and express my enthusiasm. Often this is like a slap in the face for me. I retreat to a safe distance, or ask myself how I could increase the dosage of my compliments so that at least part of them could reach their recipient. Both possibilities are reactions to a problem which, viewed superficially, may not be threatening, but in the last analysis contains the potential of self-destruction. The proclamations go: "Yeah, but in the first movement I made a mistake", "The last concert went much better", "If the audience only hadn't been so tame", "In the rehearsal I played much better", etc.

Now, there are persons who have an imagined feeling of guilt. They have a permanently operating bad conscience that works like a vehicle out of balance. This feeling is unpredictable and articulates itself in a most exaggerated way. If we do not belong to this group of people, nonetheless the sentence applies: by belittling ourselves on our own, we prevent others from doing so. We

95

would rather criticize ourselves before others can condemn us. If we turn against ourselves, we can free ourselves of our feelings of guilt, at least for a short time, and ease the bad conscience we have developed because of our heightened expectations. By invalidating others' praise, we also transmit a wishful picture of ourselves, our talents, our hidden potential, and what we would actually be capable of, if only...

A slightly more direct variant of the above tactic is the attribution of fault. "If my teacher (or coach) actually hadn't made me unsure of myself", "The room (the lighting, the acoustics, etc.) was actually working against me", "My colleagues actually gave me compunctions", "You know that it's actually impossible to be good in front of such people", etc. A particular misfortune, the colleagues, the room, or the audience—any one or all of these can be at fault if today we weren't as good as we actually could be. With all these diversionary tactics, the word "actually" plays an important role. "Actually" means "yes, *but*". It expresses the fact that we do not wish to take the responsibility for something that today was the best of our possibilities—for it truly was that; for I don't know anyone who willfully presents himself in public in a bad light. Instead, we put on a make-up of excuses and attributions of fault which may relieve us in the short term, but which in the long run will weaken us. We are thus deceiving ourselves. Besides, these evasions can become a habit requiring increasingly high doses and finally making us dependent.

The way out of these apparent maneuvers sounds simple and has nothing to do with vanity, but with simplicity. We will go further if we renounce these tactics completely. Quite simply, we should own up to what was attainable for us today. Admitting—no matter how the result may have been—that we tried our best, and that today no more was possible, also means that we get to know ourselves and to reconcile ourselves with our own possibilities, limitations, and weaknesses.

How We Set Traps for Ourselves

Self-irony, cynicism, and "the art of putting off" are associated with self-contempt; they are out of place if we want to come to terms with our fears.

Often we have only a vague notion of how we are standing in our own way. We restrict our efficiency and reduce our performance. How do we do this? What varieties are there to this game?

One of its varieties is self-irony. There is nothing we fear more than others' laughter, so we beat them to it by making jokes about ourselves. It may be that behind this posture we have the hope of fending off possible catastrophes through ridicule, cynicism, or sarcasm; but usually we only attract them. Here are a few examples of such phrases that boomerang on us: "I'll bet that I stumble when I bow to the audience", "When everything seems to be going well, the first sour note is not far away", "Wouldn't it be funny if I made a mistake just before the end", "It would be typical of me to miss the very first note", "Here comes the place where I'll probably slip".

For witnesses, such conversations with oneself might sound amusing. Unfortunately, however, this kind of irony produces just what we are intending to avoid. We really stumble at the foreseen spot, because that is what our energy is concentrated on. We really get into a cold sweat, because the envisioned situation is just about to happen. Our unconscious stores away our cynicisms and our negative prophecies, taking them literally. Irony, cynicism, and negative prophecies therefore cannot help us. The more we belittle ourselves, the greater the discrepancy between our self, which would like to be successful, and the self-destructive forces preventing us from realizing our potential. As opposed to humor, which has a freeing effect, self-irony and cynicism are associated with self-contempt. They are absolutely out of place if we want to come to terms with our fears.

Another trap we set for ourselves is our preparation. We create detours for ourselves by filling up our calendars precisely during the period just before our performance. Suddenly we find ourselves occupied with a thousand other things and hardly find the time to concentrate on the impending event. Fatigue and exhaustion are the result, and sometimes we even get the flu. Then, of course, we will have a good reason for not being able to give our best. We may have invested a lot of energy and been very active indeed, but we were just too busy with other things.

The opposite tack is less strenuous and thus more seductive; it is called "mañana, or the art of putting off". Something manages to hold us back, we feel ourselves blocked, and we have lots of good arguments for not being able to perform our task. We put our preparations "on hold" and dissipate our energies by reading magazines, making phone calls, cleaning house, cooking, or going shopping. Suddenly the date is very close and it becomes clear to us that we will hardly make it. The tricks of the mañana tactic may be self-pity—"Why do I always have to do this?" "I never have time for things that I really enjoy" —or even the dulcet tones of laziness, whispering to us: "As smart as you are, you'll be ready in time anyway", "The audience won't notice anyway", or "My concert is only out in the sticks".

All these tricks are self-erected traps, sabotaging us and causing us to fall short of our capabilities.

Chronically putting something off, however, can also be associated with our inner doubter and his companion, the perfectionist. The fear of not being able to live up to our own expectations or of risking a disaster causes us not to take the risk in the first place. In addition, as paradoxical as it may seem, the fear of success can also be a barrier. For example, if we were to succeed at something of which we ourselves or others thought ourselves to be incapable, this could requires us to change our opinion about ourselves. We might also lose the sympathy of those who either thought us not to be capable of much or otherwise had an interest in keeping us in our place. Therefore, in putting off our preparatory work and only delivering "fast food", we ensure that what we are afraid of takes place: that the others are right.

Ways Out of the Dilemma—or: Man the Maker

Taking drugs to reduce performance anxiety, besides producing certain physical effects, does not cause any progress in our self-knowledge.

In the attempt to evade performance anxiety temporarily, people have come up with a kind of progress, often developing solutions which afterwards reveal themselves to be only apparent ones, surrogates. Some believe in Erhardt Seminar Training (EST), rebirthing, or salvation through jogging or asceticism, others in autogenic training, rhetorics, or crash courses in polishing up their image. And the really smart ones: they just take miracle pills. Isn't it in fact seductive? Just a little pill, and already by chemical means we are relaxed! Besides, nobody notices when our hand dips into the little pillbox just before the event begins. This ritual alone often works wonders. Like a mighty fortress the little pill builds itself up in front of our fears, and generally the desired calmness appears without fail.

Is this the way things were meant to be? Can anything thrive in such soil? Inner feelings? Knowledge? These questions prompt me to illuminate more clearly the whole question of stage-fright drugs. I will confine myself to the so-called beta blockers, since these drugs are the most widely used in combating performance anxiety.

Beta Blockers

It is completely new in our time that we have the possibility of influencing performance anxiety via chemicals. It was only in the late 70s, and mainly in the United States, that we began to speak openly about the use of beta blockers in the treatment of performance anxiety and to direct our research in that direction. Until then, their use was rather tabooed and reserved for private experimentation. The consumption of beta blockers against such anxiety has since snowballed, so that for example in many American symphony orchestras of the 80s, only few musicians considered themselves able to get on without their beloved pills. The inexorable demands on performance skill, the pressure of time, and the existential fear of mistakes because of the threat of losing one's job have led to these pills being swallowed not only in concerts, but in rehearsals as well. Feelings of solidarity lead one to pass them on to colleagues, friends, and even to pupils who believe they can profit from them. And that is surely only the tip of the iceberg. Under its surface there are surely many more who have uncontrolled access to these drugs.

What effect do beta blockers have? In the meantime it has become known that stage fright causes the body to release certain hormones. We all have heard of the stress hormone, adrenaline. It is assumed that adrenaline stimulates mainly the so-called beta receptors of the nerve cells. When these cells are activated, they cause symptoms such as heart pounding, trembling, perspiring, or faintness—the typical signs of stage fright. From this fact, scientists deduced that performance anxiety would probably cease if they were to block these receptors with so-called beta blockers. This deduction has proven to be true: the physical symptoms of performance anxiety are dampened, one's fine motor activity is unimpaired, and one's thinking is not retarded, as is the case with tranquilizers. Thus beta blockers seem to be a useful means of coping with the physical components of performance anxiety.

The spiritual components, however, the real roots of performance anxiety, thereby remain untouched. These lie in the realm of our self-understanding, our feelings of self-worth, and our relations with our fellows. This realm, let it be stated, does not allow itself to be treated with drugs. It can only be approached when we have the courage to be in full possession of our faculties, when we see through the challenge with which our stage fright presents us, and our spirit is capable of being moved.

Although the drugs known as beta blockers can silence our inner judge and timid soul for a time, the list of disadvantages is longer. Beta blockers are dangerous for many people: for example, for those suffering from asthma, heart disease, or diabetes. This danger could be brought under control if a doctor were to be consulted in every case. In practice, however, these pills are passed on under the table regardless of the users' individual needs—see the musicians' drug, inderol. In addition, the chronic use of such drugs is habit-forming up to complete dependency, so that serious complications can follow withdrawal. Furthermore, chronic use causes the number of beta receptors to increase, so that an oversensitivity to adrenaline develops, leading to an increase in nervousness if the drug is not used. In short: frequent use causes an aggravation of the stress problem when the drug is withdrawn. Ethical problems and side effects aside, this solution reveals itself as a mere short cut. It only gives us the illusion that there is a practical solution for everything, a solution which, apart from the physical effects, does not allow any growth of our healthy self-knowledge.

All the apparent maneuvers, tricks, tactics, and short cuts mentioned above have one thing in common: we can hide behind them. We can preserve our facade and conceal our vulnerability behind a fortress of excuses. We don't bother anyone with these actions, for with them we remain adapted to the grinding wheels of humanity; but we become estranged from ourselves.

For those looking for "healthy" alternatives to beta blockers, let me disclose my house recipe for emergencies:

Mix together: 2 teaspoons of liquid lecithin
             2 teaspoons of sea-buckthorn juice*page 103
             25 drops of lemon oil

It has an effect similar to that of beta blockers, but it tastes much better and is much healthier. (However, because of the minimal percentage of alcohol in the lecithin, it is not recommended for teetotalers.) I have already mixed this recipe for many friends and acquaintances—and always with good results.

* Despite its exotic name, sea-buckthorn juice is readily available in health-food stores, at least in Germany, where it is known as *Sanddorn-Saft*. The Latin name is still more exotic: *hippophaë rhamnoides*.

6

Performance Anxiety as a Cry of the Soul

Feelings of performance anxiety are born from inner involvement and entanglement. Fear, shame, anger, and confusion are four of the most prominent feelings involved.

If we know which inner voices are our companions, influencing our thinking, now we must find out how our feelings go along with all this. For a person afflicted with performance anxiety, feelings certainly represent the most complicated realm, all the more so since feelings have the power of putting our observing ego out of commission or even overpowering it completely. First of all, feelings are the language of our involvement. They show us that we are not indifferent to our "performance", but that it means something to us. Feelings of performance anxiety are born from participation, inner involvement, and from our fascination about a coming event. Our relation to ourselves and to the world would have a totally different quality if we had no feelings, for without them we'd be robots. Feelings are thus meaningful and necessary for performance. As long as we don't know how to deal with our feelings, we might find it necessary to ignore or belittle them. In such a case, however, it behooves us to know that the essential tasks are still in front of us.

Applied to performance anxiety, this all means that we have to learn to live with these feelings, but without letting them rob us of our awareness, overwhelm us, or block us. If the attitude towards our inner voices was "let it come", then towards our feelings it basically must be: LET IT BE.

Fear

As any afflicted person can tell us, a prominent place among the feelings evoked by performance anxiety is occupied by fear. As opposed to pain, for example, which is usually confined to a specific spot, fear is total. Whoever is fearful has it from head to toe, inside and outside—fear is all-enveloping. It can express itself in various ways, as restlessness, irritability, tenseness, apathy, clumsiness, and insecurity, and via their corporeal companions such as perspiring, freezing, experiencing pressure in the heart or stomach areas, or having the desire to urinate or defecate. In any case, the presence of just a few of these symptoms will produce fear. Regardless of whether we call it hecticism, stress, nervousness, or uneasiness, nothing can change the fact that it is fear we are dealing with. By the way, the word "anxiety" comes from the Latin word *angustus*, meaning "narrow". This etymological root, together with the actual bodily sensation of narrowness or tightness, symbolizes the psychological background of fear as one of blocking, of the crossing of boundaries, or separation—as we will shortly see.

Let us remind ourselves of the feeling we had shortly

before going onstage, when we had only one wish: "Let's get away from here!" The component "away", however, is blocked, because we are inhibited by the situation, our motivation, and our role-consciousness. Now let us continue: the curtain is raised, we take a deep breath and "jump into the water". Suddenly a completely different feeling is there, and it is as though our fear had completely evaporated. Just a moment ago we tormented ourselves with battered brain and struggling heart, but suddenly we feel conviction and courage. Thus the fear which we had felt previously not only announced something—in this case, "danger: the curtain is going up"—but at the same time introduced a reaction, one directed towards overcoming the impending danger.

In this example, the fundamental polarity of our feelings becomes clear. From narrowness comes wideness. Said in a different way: when we risk "jumping into the water", fear can turn into courage.[32] If we defy fate, the frontier of fear becomes the line of battle. Nervousness becomes steadfastness, a boundary is crossed. The perspective of crossing boundaries gives fear a progressive side. Where there is fear, there is also the power of widening, and we are vibrant with the feeling of having conquered space. This presupposes that we have the courage to jump. When we jump, our blocked energies are diverted into new channels: fear becomes courage, and courage grows into trust. Trust is diametrically opposed to fear. It soothes, relieves, and widens us. However, how can we learn to make trust our ally not after going onstage, but beforehand?

Trust cannot be insinuated. It arises from the certainty that we can rely on our performance preparation. If we have prepared ourselves to the best of our ability, then we can confidently leave the rest—which is beyond our control anyway—to fate, to chance, to the gods, whatever we want to call it. In the last analysis, each successful performance is not only the result of our careful preparation, cannot be "made", then, but is also a gift given to us, a moment of grace in which we can only say, "Thank you".

Of course, things look completely different if we have not prepared ourselves properly. In this case I would speak of adaptive fear or justified fear, because now we have good reason to be afraid. If in such circumstances we are foolhardy enough to feel reliance, then it can only be according to the motto, "Somehow things will work themselves out". Such an attitude of blind trust is superficial, because it is disparaging. However, if our preparation for a performance is appropriate—and I mean appropriate and not perfect, for perfection is unrealistic—then we will be able to look our fear straight in the eye. The flaw generated by our society, then, is not fear itself, but rather our attitude to it. Fear exists and is here to stay; and instead of tormenting ourselves, fighting it, or fleeing from it, we ought to try to accept it as a harbinger of the crossing of a boundary. It is a messenger urging us on. If we can reconcile ourselves to our fear, our steadfastness and courage will grow, and we will no longer need to fear our fear. It is only through an affirmation of our fear—not by retreating because we feel sorry for our weakness—that we can cross our inner boundaries.

Crossing boundaries is an adventure, one of overcoming our self-erected barriers. First there is the barrier between ourselves and our wishes, and then there is the one between ourselves and our audience. If we isolate ourselves from our audience, separation will arise and, with it, fear. If we face our audience with feelings of mistrust or hostility, we will have to conceal ourselves; and in so doing, we thwart our desires. The opposite of this constellation is a feeling of being protected. If we feel protected, then we are at one with our audience. We receive resonance and support, and our fear can disappear.

When dealing with fear in this way, first it is important to discover: how do I impede contact with my audience? By my voice? My posture? My gestures? Here is an example from my practice. A pianist was terrified of the thought that her audience might discover how her fingers trembled. I asked her to play for our therapy group and to intensify the trembling, to play as jittery as possible. To her surprise she discovered that the trembling suddenly went away by itself. Through the permission to tremble, the energy generated by her fear had transformed itself into high-spirited playing. She then realized that her trembling had been caused principally by her wish to conceal her inner feelings from her audience. Therefore, the solution to her problem did not lie in getting control over her trembling or fighting it, but rather in opening herself up to her listeners and making contact with them. Through subsequent experiments with various ways of using her fingers as organs of contact with the audience, her playing took on a new dimension.

The fear of appearing as a failure in front of one's audience is perhaps the most frequently experienced variety of fear. It is not only past failures and negative experiences that are responsible. Past successes, too, can make us victims of the fear of failure. This type of fear, however, is often not recognized as such by those afflicted. With this type, each success causes us to alter our self-evaluation, and our demands grow. After all, to be successful means widening our concept of ourselves, taking on more responsibility, standing more in the limelight, preserving our status. The higher we raise our demands, the greater the danger of a crash.

It is typical of people imprisoned in their fear of failure that their inner judge exerts a strongly devaluating influence on them. They imagine their inner judge's self-observation to be the audience's observation. Such people feel themselves exposed to the stares of others, and these in turn are perceived as being just as critical and belittling as their own inner eye. Because in their phantasy they constantly see themselves with others' eyes, they lose reference to themselves and to their own spontaneity. The imagined "others" then become so dominating that these people feel blocked or paralyzed. The technical term for this strategy is "projection". A typical example of how people project their own belittlements onto their audience is the phrase, "They could find out that I am incompetent", which actually means: "I am afraid of my own belittling impulses, which mark me as incompetent."

The way out of these projections is always by turning them around and attributing them to ourselves. How is this done? We can dissolve projections if we have a try at accepting those character traits which bother us in others and those fears which we have ourselves, then investigating what could be true in all this. For example, a candidate for an examination who says, "The examiners are so strict", should try to empathize with the statement: "I am strict with myself". By accepting in ourselves what we fear from others, we receive the key to our own closed doors. If we stop attributing our own belittling tendencies to others, we will be able to begin taking responsibility for our own devaluating voices. In so doing, we will be able to reacquire facets of our personality.

Our predisposition towards self-belittlement can have another facet: rivalry. The more we tend to see rivals everywhere, the more susceptible we become to inadequacies and weaknesses and the more indefatigably we will compare ourselves with others. These don't necessarily have to be concrete rivals; it can be also a matter of our inner picture of perfection. There are many, especially among teachers, who are of the opinion that rivalry and fear are achievement-promoting. To be sure, there probably are people who are not sufficiently motivated for their actions without a certain amount of competition and fear. Most people, however, tend to be slowed down by anxious tension. Furthermore, I cannot imagine how it is possible to arrive at creative solutions under the whip of fear, much less develop enthusiasm for anything. In the meantime word will certainly have got around that fear is a poor teacher, because it is inhibiting.

While I was writing the above lines, a newspaper article on the violinist Gidon Kremer came into my hands.[33] It describes the psychological pressure he felt after Herbert von Karajan called him "the best fiddler we have". His crisis was intensified by the expectations of the media, who as we know live from superlatives, thereby contributing materially to the pressure applied on our favorites. Only a few are as talented as another fiddler, Anne Sophie Mutter, at adapting masterfully to society's image of success.

Entering new territory produces fear and resistance. We would rather stick to old familiar habits than risk something new. It is often just when we are performing particularly well that the fear of change overpowers us: suddenly we stumble. Who isn't acquainted with that devilish little voice whispering in our ear just after a particularly successful passage: "That can't be true—not a single mistake yet"? We know what comes next. Just when we attain something of which we had never thought ourselves capable, we hear this voice, and it makes sure that we were right. Musicians can fill entire evenings with stories about such experiences. All of them have one thing in common: that just when a concert is going particularly well, musicians are vulnerable for such mishaps. In general, it can be said that this devilish inner voice appears in just those moments when we exceed our own expectations. This little devil can seduce us to bravado, foolhardiness, or recklessness, and always with the goal of maintaining our old, limited self-concept and the familiar pastures of our self-evaluation. The safety offered by such familiarity may indeed give us some short-term relief, but we will be on a treadmill. Even though our performance anxiety may appear to be somewhat reduced by our preserving the security of the status quo, we pay a high price, for at the same time we weaken our feeling of self-worth.

We will not be able to look our fear of failure straight in the eye until we realize that the "others" actually represent projections of our own self-deprecating impulses. By the same token, we can meet our fear of success squarely if we are ready to abandon our limited self-concept, gather up the courage to allow new things to happen, and become open for new, broadening self-experiences.

Shame

Although shame is a determining factor of performance anxiety, until now it has been almost completely missing from the literature on our subject. The reason for this may lie in the complexity of the subject of shame. Shame has many faces and facets. It can show itself as timidity, an inferiority complex, inhibitions, or humiliation. A particular variant of shame is found in performance anxiety, one perceived subjectively as fear: so-called shame-fear.[34] By this is meant the fear of potential experiences causing shame or of shaming situations which could arise or could be caused by our own failure, mishap, ineptitude, or also by our having stuck our neck out too far, in other words, by exposing ourselves too much. When we expose ourselves, i. e. perform in public, questions arise. "How do I look in the eyes of the others?" "What respect do I enjoy?" "How am I evaluated?" This question as to our value or importance is the central question of shame-fear.

The more secure we feel ourselves to be as persons, the more independent we are of outside judgments and evaluations. However, if we have doubts about our self-worth, then others' evaluations take on vital importance. Being dependent on others' reactions and appraisals, we become extremely sensitive and vulnerable to even the slightest signs of rejection or indifference. "The worst thing for me is silence; when nobody tells me how good I was, then I start doubting myself and everything else." This statement made by a young cellist shows precisely where the source of shame is to be sought: in our lack of self-confidence and our feeling of self-worth. Shame, then, is based not only on the ways in which our person is evaluated or devaluated from outside, but also on the way we rate ourselves.

When we expose ourselves, we always reveal part of our intimacy, thus making ourselves more vulnerable. It makes no difference if it is with a piece of woodwork, a picture, or a musical composition. Whenever we show ourselves to others, we always direct their attention to something personal and are always putting on some kind of a show. We cannot run away and hide. In this connection, the root of the word "shame" is etymologically interesting. It derives from the Indogermanic word *kam* or *kem*, meaning "cover up", "veil", or "conceal". The wish to conceal oneself is thus indissolubly connected with shame. (This is also a reason why it became the custom in German-speaking countries to refer to one's genitals as *Scham*, shame.) Now, on what is the specific shame-fear of performance anxiety based?

Whenever we step into the limelight, there is always the danger of exposure, since we thereby allow certain aspects of our person to be illuminated which are embarrassing to us. Usually it is a matter of sensitive, intimate parts of our self, the exposure of which we particularly fear. It can be a slip of our tongue which reveals something about us or permits an insight into that "weak spot" we wished to conceal. It can also be a matter of the discrepancy between our expectations—that is, how we wish to be seen—and our appearance. Since the discovery of such a discrepancy takes place as a public exposure, our shame increases or becomes all-encompassing. All eyes seem to be staring at us, and it is as if everybody could laugh at us or make fun of us.

Shame in the limelight always indicates a conflict. We wish to show ourselves, fascinate, and impress, but at the same time our pleasure in doing so is embarrassing to us. It affects our relation to the audience as well. We want to be admired, respected, and glorified because of our deeds, but at the same time we fear that our needs can be seen through or are too obvious. After all, we don't want to appear conceited or, even worse, narcissistic. The more we resist these exhibitionistic impulses, the greater our fear. Sometimes it grows to such proportions that the only course left to us is retreat into anonymity, into not showing ourselves. Many an artistic career has failed at this very point because shame had hardened into a fortress, completely inhibiting the pleasurable wish to show oneself. If we take a closer look at this mixture of the pleasure of exposure on the one hand and shame on the other, we can see in them a certain appeal or tickle when we realize, for

113

example, how applause or praise can affect us. Most people who are not particularly used to success will react to applause in an ambivalent manner: on the one hand with signs of embarrassment, and on the other with satisfaction and true joy—shame paired with pleasure.

Shame is something natural. Its function is to veil our weakness and thus protect our identity. It is comparable to a seismograph that shows us how much we are allowed to open ourselves up and reveal ourselves. Forcing ourselves to overcome our shame means renouncing our protection. We then have only ourselves to blame if we stick our neck out too far. Our shame is a feeling that must be taken seriously, for we could be dealing with real inadequacies which we should work on before showing ourselves in public. Therefore, shame is not only the protector of our individuality. It can also be a signpost on the way to positive self-recognition, a quality which brings us forward. If we learn to hearken within ourselves, we will notice that we possess an inner voice of knowledge, a voice that gives us hints, now subtly, now quite powerfully, as to when, how, where, and if at all something is right for us. It is up to each of us to find his own balance. Both fear and shame can become our allies, if we are prepared to accept ourselves with all our strengths and weaknesses. The more tolerant we are towards our own weaknesses, the readier we will be to live with the fact that others can perceive our weaknesses and ineptitudes.

Irritation and Anger

What do irritation and anger have to do with performance anxiety? The question is justified, all the more so since at first glance the outward appearance of this affliction does not yield many criteria and furthermore, with few exceptions, the professional literature does not take a stand on this issue.[35] In fact, irritation and anger play quite an important part in our anxiety cluster—especially if we are unsuccessful in fulfilling our inner judge's perhaps unrealistic expectations and demands. Not being able to fulfil certain demands not only makes us afraid, it can also make us mad. We are angry at ourselves, angry that we feel anxious at all, even though it was we who were longing for that appearance in public. We are angry at not having prepared properly, or because we feel small and helpless. The fiercer our inner judge jacks up his demands and the more difficult it becomes to gain his approval, the more powerful becomes our conviction: "I won't make it anyway (that I am loved, etc.), so to the devil with them all!" Such aggressions directed outwards—but which in reality mask those directed inwards—can serve as a kind of antidote against fear; for when we are angry, our inner timid soul stays in hiding.

Another trigger for anger is control. If our ideal is total control or perfection, then disappointment and anger will never be far away. When we appear in public, we are particularly exposed to situations beyond our control. There are factors that affect us such as unpleasant rooms, noisy air-conditioners, acoustical imponderabilities, unpredictable disturbances, or people who do not respect our need for distance. Many performances, on the other hand, live from the fact that things are allowed to develop spontaneously. Examples of these are lectures with question and answer sessions, school recitals, or improvisation concerts. If we approach these occurrences with the pretension of total control, we will be disappointed. Dis-appointing means that our choosing ceases, and with it, our illusions. Such an illusion is our belief that it is possible to have everything under our own control or, as the phrase goes, "to get a handle on" something. If in the face of such events we allow anger to take its outward course, we become relieved.

Of course, we all know that venting anger in public is considered to be a sign of bad manners. For this reason many of us tend to direct our anger inwards, towards ourselves. However, if we do this and heap self-incriminations upon ourselves in addition —because of not being able to reach the ideal we've set for ourselves and others—then the result is self-condemnation. The condemning inner voice says, "Simply unbelievable what you're doing now—impossible". Condemnations are humiliating. They drive us into a corner, provoking irritation and anger—the voice of rebellion. We cannot fight against condemnation and win. It is like a weed: when we cut it, it just grows back even more luxuriantly. We cannot say, "I am impossible", without summoning a wave of feelings we associate with being impossible or being worthless; and we react to such feelings by becoming angry.

Awareness, as opposed to condemning, is a kind of interested and detached attention with which we observe ourselves, without forcing ourselves to go in any particular direction. Awareness changes our attitude. We are no longer victims of our anger, we can make decisions, and we can give ourselves the chance of reconnoitering the entire field of our need for control. It appears important to me that we acknowledge our anger, even greet it ("There you are again"), and allow it to express itself. In so doing, we can at the very least prevent it from coming from our unconscious and thereby unpredictably wreaking havoc. If we allow our irritation and anger to express themselves, then we will usually discover completely different feelings: reconciliation and sympathy. We all know these feelings after an argument with a person near to us. It is as if a dividing wall had dissolved, and we are able to look at each other with loving eyes once again.

Confusion

Performance anxiety often announces itself with the feeling of being confused. We feel ourselves insecure and meek, a vague feeling of uneasiness spreads, and we don't know what is actually going on inside us. Finally, when we come to feel we have a beehive in our brain and can't think straight anymore, that factor which is the subject of this chapter has settled in: confusion.

The dwelling-place of confusion is our head. This particular dweller has the talent of dispersing or clouding our perceptions and our thinking. Confusion sees to it that we become distracted from the feelings in our stomach and from our bodily tensions by pulling our combined energies into our head. In this state, we repress the feelings that terrorize and paralyze us.

Confusion is a diffuse feeling, one of wideness. Its opposites are concentration and clarity. How do we attain them? In the same way as with fear: first by allowing ourselves to be confused. Thus whenever we get that feeling of a beehive, we should greet it first. Perhaps we can even figure out a name or a symbol for this feeling, and speak to it: "Hello, there you are again! What's up? What would you like to tell me?" By carrying on an inner dialogue with this voice—one which for many of my clients is like a wild, excited, flapping bird, or for others is represented by an octopus or other huge animal with long grasping extremities—we can find out what it wants of us. We can even exaggerate our perception of this voice, in order to determine still more clearly what its purpose is. If we direct our attention to the confusion, feel it, and thus become familiar with it, something then happens which in technical terms is called "focussing": that is, our perception becomes directed like a laser beam at a target. In so doing, we produce the opposite effect of confusion. In place of diffuse, chaotic thoughts there is suddenly concentration, and our perception is focussed. Such a process is comparable to the situation when our body is inundated by bacteria and we suddenly find their seat. Through our concentration, a narrowing takes place, and the result of this process is clarity and precision. In other words: confusion can be defused and dissolved if we allow our attention to be focussed on it and to perceive it, nothing more. Our attention will thereby take on contours and direction. Its pieces and fragments will then fit themselves together, forming a picture with various parts. These can be memories, hopes, or doubts, and if we wish to refrain from evaluating them, we can just let them be. On the other hand, if we try to gain control over them, to scare them away, or to fight them, the feelings we have forced in a particular direction will always be met by a reaction in the opposite direction—and our anxiety will grow.

Facades and Masks

We erect facades and don masks which are intended to keep our real feelings covered up. The acceptance of our feelings makes it possible for blocked energy to be transformed into creative energy and power.

What many people pass off for freedom from performance anxiety is often nothing more than a shadow-play of warded-off or split-off feelings, their fortress against others' fear or laughter. When they are in the offensive, they dominate situations which others often cannot dominate at all. Even Maurice André, who in view of his spectacular successes with his trumpet could afford to speak about stage fright, says: "The best thing is not to think about it or talk about it".

By such magical thinking, we do not allow our stage fright to be seen because we are afraid that by acknowledging such counterproductive feelings, we might evoke them. In short: we are afraid of surrendering control by showing our feelings. For this reason we erect facades and don masks which are intended to keep our real feelings covered up.

One version of this kind of behavior is talking about performance anxiety, just the reverse of what is described above. I know several self-appointed experts capable of delivering perfect intellectual analyses of the problem, but I never find out what their feelings are. Their discourse remains limited to facts and bits of information, instead of sensations they have felt or experienced themselves. In other words, they try to solve problems dealing with feelings in their heads. They grab at rational explanations and search for tricks or recipes which they file away, thus hoping to avoid feelings completely. However, feelings cannot be dealt with in one's head or by one's will. They want to be perceived and experienced. Only when we have decided to regard them as our valuable companions, deserving of our attention and respect, will they bring us back the knowledge that we require to deal with them directly.

The Hunger for Success

Confusing success with fulfillment is one of the chief causes of performance anxiety.

As Horst-Eberhard Richter has impressively demonstrated in his book, *Leben statt Machen (Living Instead of Doing)*,[36] our society is preeminently one of doing instead of being. The principles upon which our world, marked by the myth of progress, is based are narrowly defined: try and try again, do and do still more, achieve, achieve, achieve. Our trying collectively to run along with the carousel of achievement and elevating outward success—as an aspired goal of life—to a dogma are among the most deeply-rooted illusions of Western culture. With this chapter, to be sure, I will not be able to remove the curse of success under which we find ourselves; but I can pose questions and offer some alternatives that could lead us out of our self-administered prison.

What is success? For me, it is a constant striving to grow, to learn, and to have a positive influence on others. Four elements are involved: being well-balanced in body and spirit, finding fulfillment in a vocation or calling, feeling the joy of life, and having relationships which sustain us. True success, then, is not a goal which is to be reached at any price. Instead it is a path which permits us to grow emotionally, spiritually, and in our corporeality. It is associated with our ability of giving life its meaning; and this is accomplished within the framework of humanity by working with, for, and in relation to others. Restricting success to a mere fixation on results—or goals such as material wealth, having traveled, or knowing many people—is a view which causes our spirit to be atrophied, because this persuasion gives us the illusion that everything can accomplished with will-power and self-control. Our wish to have everything under our control and to manipulate events according to our will, and our conviction that we can get what we want merely by exertion, will-power, and worry, only foster the fallacy that success can be "made", and that one success leads in a linear fashion to the next. Nothing could be further from the truth. If instead we search for fulfillment and growth, success will fall to us as a byproduct.

The need for fulfillment is completely different from the hunger for success. Fulfilment is not dependent on success, and success is not always associated with fulfillment. We could even say that the hunger for success arises when we neglect our need for fulfillment. Fulfilment and the enrichment of life then become replaced by greed for recognition or the quest for mammon. The compulsion to impress others and the avidity for materially visible success are perversions of vital needs. In the long run they lead into a blind alley. Common to both of these is that they are animated by fear and driven by ambition. Finally they tend to get out of control, always spinning higher and higher in the spiral of dependency, without ever having given true satisfaction. This is also the reason why many wealthy people understand more about making money than spending or enjoying it. They forget to live, because they feel—in dogged preparation for life—that they must constantly earn and accumulate. Inner satisfaction and fulfillment thus become replaced by dependency, and this knows only one word: "More!"

Confusing success with fulfillment is one of the chief causes of performance anxiety. If we are motivated by "success at any price", then fears *must* appear; because when we think in this way we will be expecting something

from others, thus becoming dependent on goals which have nothing to do with the task at hand. If we wish with our activity to arrive at something or to prove something merely in order to prop up our faltering feeling of self-worth, then we will be endangered, and it will not be difficult to make us unsure of ourselves. Driven on by our "success trip", we will then be following a mistaken concept fed by foreign, ersatz feelings, which make us dependent. If we appear in public with the intent to impress, we will be looking for something other than satisfaction or fulfillment. We will thus become slaves to our greed. We will have much more to fear than if our appearance were dedicated to the goals of seeking satisfaction and fulfillment, and of sharing our knowledge or ability with others in order to enrich our lives. There is a great difference if we are performing in order to attain some sort of reward, fame, or glory —that is, something lying outside the actual task—or if we are following an inner need for self-expression and growth, one which tends to be self-perpetuating, independently of what we want to attain in the future.

If we are open for learning and growing, instead of trying to prove something, then the differentiation between "what I wish for myself" and "what I need for my life" can become an important signpost. This differentiation has nothing to do with semantic hair-splitting. To the contrary: if we live only according to the principle of "what I wish for myself" or "what I would like", we will often find ourselves following the dictates of our resistance to growth. For somebody who feels most at ease in his cozy little room, for example, "what I wish for myself" would mean loneliness, while what he really needs for growth would be to practise self-confidence among other people. However, if we follow the path of "what I need", then we will find ourselves on the way to learning and becoming whole. This path is certainly not always comfortable, but it is worth the effort. Everyone knows this who has not capitulated before the fear of showing himself in public, but, having remained steadfast in the face of fear, has experienced new self-trust as a result and as a reward.

If we follow the path of "what I need", we will quickly be able to unmask the greed for success. This is because we probably will notice that our thirst for fulfillment cannot be quenched by applause. Furthermore, we will notice that behind our greed for success there is always another, deeper lack, one requiring another kind of nourishment. Add to this the fact that the goals we are pursuing will not remain hidden to our environment. Our inner attitude affects not only ourselves, but our audience as well. This has to do with the fact that we are constantly communicating. Our phantasies, thoughts, and feelings— our inner communication—are always directed outwards as well. What we imagine, what we intend, what we say to ourselves, how we use our body—all of this transmits itself to the outside. Therefore, in the last analysis we cannot conceal it if we are using our audience in order to impress. Conversely, our audience will also sense it if we radiate joy, enthusiasm, and love because we are fulfilled by our task. And what is still more important: the degree of fulfillment that we feel inside ourselves is the result of how we communicate with ourselves.

7

Our Inner Allies

In the search for performance power, it is necessary to know how we can employ our nourishing, sustaining resources for ourselves.

Now that we have illuminated the various moods and feelings characteristic of performance anxiety, you will probably have recognized a few components of your own anxiety landscape. However, we do not only possess inner voices which tighten, afflict, or torment us. We also dispose of inner allies founded in positive experiences of our past, in scenes in which we were given courage, encouragement, and consolation. We do not internalize only the dark side of our most important role models, but their sunny side as well. Unfortunately, in many kinds of therapy, too little attention is paid to the latter side because of a one-sided treatment of elements hampering us. Our helpful inner resources often escape our glance because we take them for granted, therefore not paying sufficient attention to them, and because we have not been well enough informed as to how we can employ our nourishing, sustaining qualities for ourselves.

To find our performance power, I believe it to be of fundamental importance that we also get acquainted with the voices of our inner allies and to have them at our disposal in difficult situations. Three voices play a role here: our inner mentor, the voice of trust, and that of curiosity.[37]

Our Inner Mentor

Our inner mentor will be a valuable companion if we decide to lead a life involving other people and things.

This inner voice is benevolent; it is our friend and adviser. Our mentor is acquainted with our strengths and weaknesses and wants the best for us. As opposed to the inner perfectionist or the judge, he will offer us esteem and support, qualities we need above all when we approach decisions, have problems to solve, or simply seek advice and assistance. As opposed to the perfectionist, he orients himself towards what is possible: that is, towards attainable goals. Our mentor knows that each step on the way to a goal is already a success. His knowledge rests on the experience we have acquired during the course of our life, and on an understanding of our possibilities and limitations. We can count on him when we are looking for ways to better ourselves and to make progress, for his advice is marked by benevolence and esteem. If we occupy ourselves with the question, "What do I have to learn in this phase of life?", with his help we will be able to determine where we feel ourselves to be stuck and to find out what the next step should be. Our mentor appeals to our own healthy resources and forces. For him, failures do not exist. There are only results—those we can attain, those from which we can learn, and those which we can also change. Among our mentor's strategies are encouragement, discipline, and empathy. His doctrine can be summed up in three points: trust the wisdom of your body, relax your mind, and concentrate on the perception of what is going on right now. These attitudes will contrast with the harshness of our inner perfectionist, the false pity of our timid soul, or the inexorability of our inner judge.

Our inner mentor will be a valuable companion if we decide to lead a life involving other people and things. By this I mean goals leading us beyond ourselves to higher things. It is essentially a matter of the plain and sober question: "What do I want?" and of our concrete realization of its answer, for which I should be open at the moment of the asking.

Again and again I hear the phrase: "I would like to ..." In reality this generally means: "I believe that I would like this or that, but I won't do anything to attain it". This attitude is undisciplined and derives from the fact that many people associate the word "discipline" with deprivation, obstinacy, and commands involving the words "thou shalt". Commands create inner resistance. If we say "thou shalt" to ourselves, our unconscious interprets these words to mean: "Actually, I'd rather not". If we truly were to want something, we would never say "thou shalt"; we'd simply go for it. Discipline is the key to the gateway of our goals and is not to be confused with self-chastisement. With discipline, we have a technique for transforming wishes into wished-for fulfillment. Without discipline, we can only gaze at our wishes and dreams as if they were show windows. We gaze at them and then walk on, because we lack the means to realize what we want. Instead of self-denial, discipline means self-fulfillment. This has nothing to do with control, but rather with letting go of control and venturing into something bigger than ourselves which brings us further than our timid little ego. In the last analysis, this means: away from our tiny fearful ego, on to the job.

Our inner mentor is responsible for two kinds of problems in particular. The first is our lack of knowledge about paths leading to certain solutions; and the second is our inner barriers, preventing us from solving a given problem despite our knowledge. As far as the field of performance anxiety is concerned, there are any number of books containing patent recipes, all of them revolving around the single question: "How can I get rid of my performance anxiety?" All of them have in common the fact that they do not take our inner resistance enough into account, thus perpetuating the error that this problem can be solved with willpower and elbow grease. Instead of constantly asking, "How?" we should try with our inner mentor's help to discover which sorts of resistance there are that prevent us from appearing before our audience relaxed and self-confident. If we can learn to accept both our resistance and its value for us, then it will become known to us and, with this, changeable. Then we can stop our feverish search for the "how" and direct our attention to the much more important question of "Why not?". Fritz Perls once compared the problem of resistance with that of tensing a muscle; if we can feel that it is tensed, we can also learn to relax it.

The Voice of Trust

It opens the gateway to belief in ourselves.

Goethe's admonition, "Earn it so as to own it", is of great importance, especially concerning our trust in ourselves. It means no less than the fact that we first must build up trust, if we wish to have it at our disposal. This implies that everything we do must rest on a solid foundation. This in its turn will become capable of supporting us—not by blind faith, but only through conscientious work, thorough preparation, and regular practice of our skills. If we have once acquired control over our skills, then we will also be able to surrender it. Such letting go can lead to magic moments, ones in which people exclaim with wonder, "The music was playing me", "I was completely at one with my entire surroundings", "It was like a third power", "a peak experience". These utterances hint at something of the secret of trust. Trust arises not only from our knowledge or ability, but also through our recognition of the possibility that we could fail. If we can allow ourselves to fail, then something paradoxical will happen: we will no longer need to trust in being successful. The more we can allow the possibility that both could happen—success or failure—the less we will need to reflect on trust at all.

Our inner voice of trust opens the gateway to belief in ourselves. As such, it is the opposite of our inner doubter, sabotaging us with uncertainty and confusion. What we believe and consider to be possible largely determine what we are able to do—or not to do. An American proverb states: "Whether you believe that you can do something or that you can't, you'll always be right". When we speak of believing, we usually think of dogmas; but in the original meaning of "belief", any conviction, attitude, or passion is a belief giving direction to our life. Our inner belief helps us to tap our healthy inner resources and to employ them for our paths and goals. Belief in ourselves is not only a compass for our goals, but it also gives us the necessary guarantee of reaching them.

Many people think belief to be a rigid intellectual concept having no relation to our actions or experience. The opposite is true. It is precisely because our believing is closely bound up with our actions and our experience—

since the path to belief is at first paved with questions, doubts, or disbelief—that we can say that it is not something absolute, but is rather a flexible product of our potential's coming to terms with the tasks set for us.

Our belief in ourselves can give us wings and protect us. It is the sum of all the positive experiences we have had during the course of our lives. In my work with clients, I often pose the question: "In what quality in yourself can you trust?" Since we occupy ourselves much more often in our daily lives with things that inhibit us, their first reaction is often embarrassment and hesitation. However, if it becomes clear to us that we have inner resources that often remain hidden away because we have not been sufficiently encouraged to deal with them, then calmness and clarity always appear, and with them the insight that we can choose our belief ourselves. It is in our power to choose a belief that supports us. Moreover, we will reach our goals much more easily if we believe in ourselves. Such a belief can guide us like the north star. This means that we should become clear in our minds and allow our belief in our own capabilities to have a magnetic effect, steering our energies in a particular direction.

Of course, this does not mean that we will be automatically free of performance anxiety if we simply believe steadfastly in ourselves. However, it can at least cause us not to run away from our fears, because we can trust in something within ourselves which is stronger than fear—our belief in ourselves. Even though today or tomorrow we may be plagued by fears or doubts, with the help of our inner voice of trust we can at least stop lamenting: "Never", as in: "I'll never succeed" or "I'll never be able to make it", etc.

The Voice of Curiosity

This is the creative voice within us responsible for joy, humor, and adventure.

Listening to this inner voice means gaining self-confidence. It is the opposite pole of what our inner timid soul is responsible for, that is, adjustment or flight. Like our inner mentor, this voice is also interested in our personal growth, but its procedure is different. It encourages us to try things out, to seek change, and to take risks. This is the creative voice within us. It is full of the joy of discovery and new ideas, and is always on the lookout for individual solutions. For me personally, my voice of curiosity is my most important ally, because it induces elements such as joy, humor, and adventure into the serious business of appearing in public. Above all, it is free of prejudices and preconceived expectations. It is responsible for surprises and brings about relaxation, because its attitude is something like: "Well, how is the trip going to be today?"

It is through our curiosity that we make contact with the inner child we once were. Do you remember? As children we didn't have any learning problems. We made adults look silly when it came to discovering, investigating, or assimilating new things. As children we were inquisitive. (The German word for this speaks volumes: *neugierig* = *neu-gierig* = "new-greedy" = "greedy for new things".) We were enthusiastic, bewitched, and fascinated by all the possibilities of getting to know our bodies, of rehearsing new potentialities of expression, and of conquering the world of objects. How does the typical adult produced by our society look? He seems to belong to quite another race, because he has exchanged his "greed for things new" for so-called normality.

As adults, we hold in our hands the potential of reacquiring our joy of discovery, our inquisitiveness. Slumbering inside us, it is practically crying out to be allowed to live and learn once again. It is not something new that we would have to learn, but rather something that many of us have forgotten. When we approach a public appearance with curiosity, something more happens: we experience feelings of pleasure, our body pulses with vitality, our imagination takes wings, and our senses awaken. The discoveries we make with the help of our curiosity do not have to be grandiose. They must neither last for eternity nor be constantly new. A witty introduction for a lecture, a striking piece of clothing, or a more conscious posture will often suffice in effectuating a change in our attitude towards our audience. The real issue is that we experience our performance with feelings of pleasure and understand it to be a learning situation. If our actions are imbued with curiosity, our radius of living will be expanded. Then we will understand something of what Kierkegaard meant when he spoke of the "giddiness of freedom"—that interpenetration of fear, courage, and joy we feel when we suddenly discover our inner strength.

The voice of curiosity is one of the best companions we have within us. It can serve as a bridge for us to cross over from fear to courage, because it sees its chance when we stand up to our fear. Even though we may sometimes be trembling as we make our way forward, it will spur us on, because there are so many things to discover. Perhaps this sounds superficial. However, for our inner voice of curiosity, the final issue is to discover our inner strength. We will only discover this strength if we can also acknowledge our vulnerability. Finally, in our vulnerability lies our personal truth and—our strength. One of the secrets of performance anxiety is that it will release us from its grip if we are ready to admit and accept our vulnerability.

8

Ways Out of Performance Anxiety

We must enter into the paradox of gaining an increase in self-confidence by reconciling ourselves with our vulnerability.

We will not be able to take a single step away from our anxiety and towards performance power if we occupy ourselves with mere words, remaining at a safe distance by reading books. This attitude is familiar to me from my work with many persons so afflicted. They expect me to pronounce the magic word of deliverance or to produce the healing "aha effect", instead of entering into what they feel and experience themselves. It is not a matter of reading interesting facts about performance anxiety in general, but rather of having a look at one's own individual performance-anxiety profile, confronting it, and while in this attitude of involved observation, of gathering experience and venturing new steps. We must enter into the paradox of gaining an increase in self-confidence by reconciling ourselves with our vulnerability.

This realization is connected with the insight that our feelings are in motion between two poles. Each one of our feelings moving in a certain direction also evokes its opposite. This means that if a part of us is very conservative and opposed to change, then its opposite will also exist: that part which has some notion of motion and wants to go ahead. That part in us which is sensitive to performance anxiety will perhaps try to protect us in the best possible way that it knows. However, it also will bring us into contact with its opposite, the courage of standing up to our anxiety, an attitude making us ready for new experiences. These are our steps to freedom, to our performance power.

What are these individual steps? We will deal with them in the next chapter. Beforehand I would like to round off the present discussion by dealing with another kind of experience, one belonging to a completely different dimension from that of the inner voices and feelings mentioned before.

Moments of Illumination

If we are prepared to expand our consciousness, entrusting ourselves to the messages of our unconscious, an infinite number of possibilities for learning will be at our disposal.

There is a state in which our capability of perception is intensified, we experience a feeling of being at one with or of melting into what we are doing, and we feel ourselves to be a vessel of a message or an instrument of our spirit. No longer are we spectators, separated from what we are doing; we become what we are doing. In such moments of illumination, performance and performer become one. That is, we become music, movement, dance, or message. Even though such occurrences are not commonplace, we have all experienced such moments, those in which our inner gates suddenly are opened wide and we have the feeling as if

something were flowing from us or bubbling upwards as from a deep spring. Some people have reported on feeling in such moments as if something had come over them from somewhere outside themselves, some sort of power or a completely different being. Our language has an entire palette of expressions to describe such states. We speak of encountering a higher power, our higher self, inspiration, or a divinity within us. Whatever we may wish to call it, we do not have to be religious to pay heed to such extraordinary moments. What we hold to be possible and whatever we call it will depend on what we have learned to think of as possible, or what we are capable of considering to be possible. At the very least, we all have been witnesses of the fruits of such experience if we have attended a breathtaking concert, followed a spectacular achievement in sports, or listened to a speech during which we suddenly sensed a flash of illumination.

Perhaps what we call a moment of illumination has something to do with the attitude we bring to the stream of spiritual experience. This would mean that we not only leave the transient nature of such moments to chance, but that we should occupy ourselves with them and pay more attention to them. It is certainly no accident that in our time, scholars from the most diverse areas from computer science to quantum physics are discussing this very subject with great intensity. Even though they have not yet produced any unified theory concerning this phenomenon, they are already in agreement that we will have to change and expand radically our opinions about the nature of human capabilities, motivations, and inhibitions.

If we were to summarize what people have said about such moments, then certain main ideas can be extracted which are meaningful for our subject. Whoever has heard such personal reports is confronted unquestioningly with the fact that we have a dimension inside ourselves which with a paradoxical formulation I will call both our "higher self" and our "deepest foundation", one constantly observing all the other parts within us. This higher self, our deepest foundation, is the dimension in us transcending all other polarities. It is the source of our creativity, a kind of deep intuition or wordless knowing that simultaneously comprises past, present, and future. It is our all-encompassing, loving, wise, and empathic self. In moments when we abandon ourselves completely to a matter or concentrate intensively on something, by acting from inside our hearts or by receiving creative insights, we are already in contact with our higher self, our deepest foundation.

This brings up the question: is there a way for everybody to dial the wave-length of this inner experience, and how can we listen to it? At the outset, we must trust in the fact that inside us there is a kind of inner knowledge, one greater than our normal daily consciousness. The best method of tapping this inner knowledge is hearkening inwards. Let us remember Descartes' dreams, August Kekulé's snake dream, Elias Howe's nightmare, or geniuses like Edison or Einstein, whose revolutionary inventions were not due primarily to the conscious part of their spirit, but to their talent of hearkening inwards. The possible paths of such illuminations and their effects vary from person to person. They all have in common the fact that they are always preceded by consciously initiated preparatory work; and as the result of this work process, like a bolt from the blue, something new comes to light as if out of nowhere. This state comes as a surprise and without warning. It cannot be produced by a sheer act of will. Most people associate it with the metaphor of flowing. This is not only a suitable metaphor; it also intimates that in this state we have free access to dimensions whose gates are normally shut. Our daily consciousness, preoccupied with activity and control, is not attuned to them.

The capability of hearkening inwards is slumbering in all of us and is just waiting to be awakened. First, as we already know, it is a matter of learning to trust in our higher self. All of us at some time or other have heard an inner whisper, or were suddenly conscious of an inner idea, a symbol or picture, that was trying to tell us something. I am thinking here of the example of a musician who suddenly heard an inner voice as if from afar, saying, "Trust your message", or of another one who had a vision within her body of light which she was supposed to pass on to other people. If we can learn to hearken inwards, ideas and visions differing from those of our normal reality will appear. If we are prepared to accept these inner processes and images, then we will have taken a giant step in the direction of greater creativity. There is no recipe for such experiences, and no tortuous practice of meditation is required to initiate access to discoveries of this kind. The clearer, more focussed, and more concentrated our preparations for performance are, the better will be the conditions under which our unconscious will answer to them, as long as we do not disturb its workings.

Here I come to the third essential step in my performance-power formula which up to now has consisted of "let it come" and "let it be". It is LET IT GO.[38] At a certain point during any preparation for a performance, we must leave the various ingredients alone and let them simmer. This means we have to surrender control, let go, turn off, and turn the work over to our unconscious, so that our intuition, slumbering in the depths, has the possibility of becoming active through us. A kind of deep intuition seems to know the path of our maturing and of our healthy integration, simply waiting for the opportunity of leading us gently in that direction. A well-known example is the famous cry of "Eureka!" ("I've found it!") attributed to Archimedes, who solved his problem when he climbed into his bathtub and it overflowed. Suddenly, in a flash, he knew the answer. A prerequisite of this eureka effect is the conscious, clear, complete, and goal-directed preparatory work with which we program our unconscious mind.

Since our brain is not a computer, which one only needs to feed with pure factual data so that the right result comes out, but works in an infinitely more sophisticated manner, even by challenging much more complex scenarios to unfold, it is worthwhile to prepare a performance as intensively and in as many ways as possible on the emotional level, even taking peripheral matters such as room, clothing, and time of day into careful consideration, so that optimally we may tap the available archives of our entire knowledge. This process is comparable with pregnancy, at the end of which, after an intensive phase of preparation, there is LET IT GO, or just letting go.

Our unconscious will be able to occupy itself with our task with the least disturbance if we surrender control or give ourselves over to it with various methods of letting go such as deep relaxation, daydreams, or even sleep. It is then that we open ourselves to the energies of our higher self. To become receptive to its messages can be learned. This is done by practice, by consulting our unconscious frequently, with awareness, and by utilizing this information. If we can for once ignore our society's still-existing taboo, be ready to widen our consciousness, and give ourselves over to the experiences of the unconscious in order to direct them to a goal, then a myriad of possibilities for learning will become available to us, together with the proper tools, matters of which we may have been collectively aware for centuries, but which are slowly being rediscovered only recently.[39]

Pleasurable Anticipation

Performance anxiety will be transformed into pleasurable anticipation if we open our consciousness to what we are doing and are no longer blinded by the wish to possess.

Writing this book has much in common with the way we solve our problems of performance anxiety. I could allow myself to be driven by the fear that I will never make it unless I force myself to it; or I can be convinced that I will write it, even though it sometimes is not easy for me. Both alternatives require discipline and effort. We have the choice of deciding on one of the two paths. In the last analysis, our decision is associated with two questions: "How would I like to live my life?" and "Do I want myself to be driven by fear, or do I want to trust in myself?"

Self-confidence and performance anxiety, to be sure, seem to contradict each other, but both originate in the same source: our personal involvement in our actions. Without involved interest in our performances and enthusiasm for them, we probably would not have any performance anxiety—but we'd have less self-awareness and self-confidence as well. It is worthwhile to realize that the etymological root of "enthusiasm" is *"en theos"*, that is, "God within". For me, this means that the energy responsible for our enthusiasm and our involvement is nourished by our higher self. Graf Dürckheim mentions in this connection a participation in a greater life that lives within us: our being.[40] If we are at one with our being, we can bridge the gulf between the various parts of our consciousness. These are the moments which I have described above as those of illumination—our peak experiences, in which we feel ourselves at one with ourselves and the world, no longer estranged.

What do these reflections have to do with performance anxiety? The energy of our performance anxiety, too, derives lastly from the source of our higher self. However, it becomes deformed by our ego, intent on recognition and success, if we place our being in the service of "wanting to have" and "wanting to have more". If we are prepared to abandon our ego's excessive demands, we can open the gates to our higher self. They can be opened most readily when we are at the center of our action, when we are in tune with ourselves, or when we can give ourselves up to our action as do children. Then our action will correspond to our being and not to any sort of alienated goals. In such moments of being, everything is confluent, our thoughts, our feelings, our body. We have neither too much nor too little awareness—we are in a state of natural gracefulness. This condition is beyond all polarities, because then we are no longer seekers; for giving ourselves up to our action makes self-discovery and transcendence possible. A converging and integration of the forces that become revealed in our higher self or on a higher level: these are the goal of our journey. A journey of constant approaching, one which could unite the two sisters, Fear and Self-Confidence, once again.

If we realize that our performance anxiety and our self-confidence form a natural polarity, both of which are nourished from the source of our giving ourselves over to a matter, then we have taken a step in the direction of integration. If above and beyond this both these elements— self-confidence and performance anxiety—flow together and become transformed as an expression of our self, then something is generated which I consider to be the essence of fulfillment. Fulfilment arises when we give ourselves wholeheartedly to something, lose ourselves in it, and thus truly find ourselves: when we open ourselves to a truth greater than ourselves. If we surrender ourselves, we are no longer isolated, but instead we are capable of recognizing and experiencing totality: the entire universe, nothingness, the fullness of God—whatever term we wish to use for totality.

Summary of Part One

If we consider performance anxiety once again in retrospect, we see that we have have come to realize that it has various strata: the stratum of the inner voices and thoughts, where we came to recognize performance anxiety as causing us to become out of balance and to feel insecure; the stratum of feelings and resistance with which we seek to explain away, to deny, or to hush up our fears; and the stratum leading to the core of our self. By giving ourselves up to our action, one emerging from our being, we come into contact with what we are. The path leading us from "wanting to have" and "wanting to appear", into a world in which we find fulfillment—our true abode—in being, is at the same time a path transforming our performance anxiety into that quality which it ought to be: ANTICIPATION, pleasurable anticipation of a coming event in which we have involved our entire being because it has meaning for us. Performance anxiety will be transformed into anticipation if we open our consciousness to what we are doing, and not to what we want to have. Whoever accepts himself and is wholly at the center of his action or his motion will also be able to expose himself to the risk of not having to please at any price. Whoever has established his true self will absolutely no longer have to "become established".

With the transformation of performance anxiety into anticipation, we intend a qualitative change in a person's relation with himself, his fellows, and the world, one in which there is a continuous encountering, recognizing, and opening of oneself. It is a lifelong process of constantly exceeding one's ego, a process to which each one of us is required to commit himself in his own unique way if he is not to swim against the stream of life or to be engulfed by it.

The secret of this path lies in giving, not in wanting to have. All the golden calves of recognition, career, and achievement, which we often dance around to the point of exhaustion, adhere to us, choke us, and act as a magnet for more of the same. A well-known truth is: "The world is perhaps not just, but it is precise". We get what we expect.

As long as we cling to the optical illusions of the profit and loss system, we will be constrained to live in the shadow of our fears, with no chance of becoming what we could be. We will win, or lose, and in this way perhaps get hold of a few things, but behind all this, our true self will starve. Inner peace can only come to us if we are prepared to sacrifice our golden calves and become givers. An attitude of giving or giving ourselves does not mean that we become poor. To give ourselves over to an action means letting go of what we have to defend or what we seek to get hold of, being vulnerable, and letting what and who we really are shine through. It also means giving up exaggerated self-criticism and self-doubt. As soon as we let them go, criticism from outside will also diminish. If we can reconcile ourselves with ourselves, our fears will no longer be able to throw us off course. Inner peace is one's alliance with one's spiritual self and also contains humility—a term which might sound old-fashioned today. I like this expression because it is useful in describing an attitude coming from the heart and not from the conceited ego. Humility is that quality which allows us to become open, to receive. Behind this openness is not a lack of self-confidence, but rather a strong belief in oneself.

With the readiness to be a giver, together with the inner attitude of peace, our performance anxiety takes on another dimension, one in which it is no longer a matter of fighting or having to win, but of alliance with higher spiritual energies. Instead of assuming a posture of fighting, which strains us and makes us tense, we ally ourselves with the flowing energy of joy, which opens us and makes us free. And last but not least: don't forget to laugh! If we slip up, blurt out a malapropism, or stumble, it is nothing less than human and grounds for smiling. The gift of humor gives us perspective and makes us wide; it is one of the most important gateways to self-love. So laugh from time to time!

Performance Power

PART TWO: PERFORMANCE POWER

Performance Power

9

Practical Suggestions for Developing Performance Power

Performance anxiety gives us signals for possibilities of learning in the area of our personality.

In this chapter, we will become familiar with various practical considerations and coping techniques helpful in dealing with performance anxiety and leading to performance power. Different people require different strategies, and not every coping strategy will help in every situation. What functions well in one particular situation might not help at all under different circumstances. Since performance anxiety is a holistic phenomenon, with consequences for our thoughts, our feelings, and our body, a single technique is usually insufficient. It is therefore advisable to be acquainted with several possibilities, in order to react flexibly to our various ways of behavior and, depending on the situation, to find out what is most appropriate.

Fundamentally, there are two methods of dealing with performance anxiety: concentrating on making an impression, or being congruent with our being. The first one aims at polishing our personal performance to a high lustre.

For example, we can learn professional techniques of communication by taking communication training or rhetoric courses, we can practise gaining an adroit and secure appearance, making an impression while maintaining a cool head, having an optimal effect and selling ourselves, etc. Numerous books have appeared in recent years devoted to strengthening the impression we make, and their titles are indeed seductive: *Never Be Nervous Again, Never Again Stage Fright, The Power Principle, The Performance Edge, You Are a Natural Champion, The Inner Winner*, etc. In my opinion, the promises such works imply are only superficial. They veil the inherent conflicts, because they transmit the illusion that with a few recipes and tricks, a little make-up and masquerade, it is possible to correct personality problems. To be sure, with clever technologies we can polish our facade. However, when we are trained only to make an impression, we become alienated from ourselves and from others. The roots of performance anxiety thereby remain untouched; for their source lies not in maximizing our appearance, but in self-perception and dealing with our own self-concept.

Now, I do not wish to create the impression that we should be careless about the impressions made by our onstage appearance, for as soon as we appear anywhere, we are already creating an impression. In other words, we are certainly responsible for our appearance as well. After all, by our performance we wish to attain something. As long as we do not elevate our appearance to an end in itself or allow it to become autonomous, attention to our appearance certainly is justified—in order to support our self-expression and the sympathy accorded to us by our fellows.

My approach has as its point of departure a holistic idea of man. It is oriented towards being congruent, and thus its tendency is rather a therapeutic one. I am fascinated by the thought that performance anxiety is not an isolated symptom of some kind of deviation but, as the expression of an individual life, is embedded in a person's entire situation. From this point of view performance anxiety takes on its value for us. It represents valuable messages emerging from the treasure chest of our unconscious and therefore, in the last analysis, signifies an invitation to change the course of our personal life. For this reason, it is worthwhile to hearken into ourselves, asking: what does my performance anxiety reveal to myself about my life?

We have many tools for discovering the signification and the personal meaning of performance anxiety. They all have in common that we accept first of all that we have this affliction and also be willing to admit it. By such an admission, we will eliminate the pressure of having to hide such anxiety or fight against it. We will also reduce our fear of having our facade of self-confidence damaged.

Freeing ourselves from our performance anxiety is bound up most decisively with the way our self-perception is focussed. The issue is to figure out what is going on within us, consciously observing and taking mental notes of all the signals our performance anxiety sends us. By such focussing, we can transform our anxiety from a fear-producing, irrational phenomenon to an interesting object of research which we can regard with curiosity. With this attitude, performance anxiety takes on a quality of invitation for learning: that is, it will give us signals for possibilities of learning in the area of our personality.

Our Body Is Our Garden

Physiology is one of the most powerful tools to change the manifestations of performance anxiety in the

shortest possible time.

Until now, we have spoken of performance anxiety first and foremost in connection with thoughts and feelings. We have learned that certain inner attitudes and postures produce various bodily symptoms of performance anxiety, because they send messages to our brain and our nervous system. However and vice versa, our body also influences our thinking and feeling. Studies which are now beginning to become known deal with how our facial expression influences the way we feel. For example, they come to the conclusion that smiling and laughing start up biological processes—such as an increase in the oxygen concentration in the blood, improved circulation to the brain, and the release of neurotransmitters—causing us actually to feel better. Expressing irritation or anger is a similar case: assume an angry expression, and you will feel that way, too.

By now it has certainly become clear that the effects of performance anxiety can either further our concentration and improve our achievement or else be a burden, hampering and inhibiting. In general it can be said that an increase in arousal produces a corresponding increase in performance level, until an optimal level of arousal is reached. If arousal exceeds this level, performance can dramatically decline. Yerkes and Dodson's research from 1908 has scientifically demonstrated this connection.[41]

It is, then, a matter of finding our optimal arousal level or, in other words, that quantity of tension necessary for a desired achievement, so that we are neither too much nor too little aroused. This optimal arousal level is perceived differently by every person and varies also according to the task at hand. David Pargman, who has dealt extensively with this subject, emphasizes that there is for every person an optimal level of arousal necessary to achieve the best possible performance.[42] For gross motor skills such as throwing a discus or lifting weights a higher level of physiological arousal is necessary in order to augment the power and endurance of the large groups of muscles involved and to arrest muscle fatigue than for example with fine motor skills depending on small muscle activity and emphasizing accuracy. Thus is explained the obvious aggression prevailing in many a locker-room just before a game. Foot-stomping, rhythmic singing, and shouting are supposed to intensify arousal in preparation for the confrontation, because it is assumed that a high level of arousal is necessary for the attainment of top form.

On the other hand, if we were to observe a pianist just before he goes onstage, we would see a completely different picture. Perhaps he is in the process of meditating, or is relaxing himself with autogenous training. He will avoid arousing himself, because he knows that he must stay calm if he is to attain an optimal performance. This insight is easy to confirm. Try sometime after a heated debate to perform a fine motor skill such as sewing on a button. You will probably see that you need several tries and much more time than if you were to perform the same action after having listened to meditative music.

To sum up: gross motor skills require a higher degree of physiological arousal than fine ones. A gross-motor person will thus tend towards methods of activity increase aimed at setting his bodily chemistry in motion, such as activating self-conversations, energetic movement, stimulation from outside, or animating music, whereas the fine-motor person will be better served by techniques of relaxation and autosuggestion. However, to determine precisely what the required degree of arousal should be for a given activity is extremely difficult, since each one of us must find his own level of arousal, the one beneficial to him personally. This presupposes that we become acquainted with our personal preferences and be receptive to the signals coming from our body. Learning to deal with performance anxiety means learning to interpret our own bodily reactions and developing the skills necessary for neutralizing its blocking effects.

Physiology is one of the most powerful tools we possess to change the manifestations of performance anxiety in the shortest possible time. If we change our physiology—our posture, our breathing, and our muscle tonus—then we are also changing our emotional state. The better we treat our body, the better our brain will function. This insight is the basis of the work done by Moshe Feldenkrais, who discovered that by working in the kinesthetic area it is possible to change the condition of one's soul and spirit. In his opinion, the quality of our experience depends on the quality of our movements.[43]

There are two possibilities for dealing with the bodily symptoms produced by performance anxiety: we can either weaken, reduce, and neutralize them, or we can intensify and accentuate them. An important component is the personal feeling of being "in tune". For example, if our knees are shaking from fear and we try to persuade ourselves that we're "perfectly calm", then we are not in tune.

All of us certainly know the feeling of being out of tune: it is when one part of us wants one thing and another part balks. Being in tune means to go along with the feeling of the moment. Our body, words, and actions must correspond to one another.

Coping with Bodily Symptoms of Performance Anxiety

The process I call LET IT COME, LET IT BE, LET IT GO can also be applied to the way we treat our bodies.

I already treated this process in the section on dealing with inner voices and feelings; it is one which can also be applied to the way we treat our bodies. LET IT COME means perceiving ourselves deeply, just as we are right now. Instead of pushing for change in order to repress certain symptoms, it is much more useful to observe them, allow them to exist, and to perceive them more deeply. The idea is to get in touch with the way our bodies are feeling, and to perceive what there is that could be waiting to be discovered. You thus ask yourself in a given moment before going "onstage": What kind of a feeling do I have in my body? You are probably feeling some kind of excitement. Your heart is pounding, you feel tense, or you have butterflies in your belly. You are probably experiencing these feelings as unpleasant, fear-provoking, or simply as a weakness. Instead of labelling them negatively like this, try instead to accept them as arousal and to perceive them still more clearly. Observe your arousal with curiosity; perhaps you can even enjoy this feeling a little. All the energy which would otherwise be blocked by resistance against the various bodily effects now becomes available for participation in what is going on in your body.

The second step, LET IT BE, means identification with our experience here and now and leads to an intensification of this experience. Belonging to this is the feeling that this is my own personal experience, whether I like it or not. The bottom line is: "This is me, and this is the way I am." In order for a given experience to become more marked or accentuated, we should exaggerate it. That is, exaggerate or strengthen each sensation of tension, uneasiness, or agitation. Instead of trying to lessen tensions, we thus perform exactly the opposite action: we exaggerate them. For example, if you feel your hands trembling, intensify the trembling. When you feel muscle tension, increase the tension in the respective muscles for a time. If you have cold hands, concentrate your thoughts on making them still colder. We can deepen this experience of intensification further by giving the symptoms still more room to express themselves. Stay in contact with the symptoms and try to stimulate them by movement, or let them converge into a kind of vocal expression. Hum some kind of tones, sounds, or noises expressive of what is inside you. In so doing, don't hesitate to exaggerate the sound; this will make the experience more intensive.

Intensification of symptoms means identifying ourselves with our experience and accentuating it: we acknowledge that this is our experience, and we deepen it. Through intensification, we are no longer victims of a particular feeling or state. Instead, we can deal with it, play or experiment with it. Thus we place ourselves in a position of involved distance, one in which we can observe our performance anxiety from afar. This means occupying an off-center position to our feelings, so that they are no longer able to overwhelm or inundate us.

The third step, LET IT GO, leads to a letting go of tensions. Our goal is not complete relaxation, which can only be reached by a state of absolute repose. We are trying for an appropriate, loose tension, one that means neither limpness nor tightness: wide-awake, energetic release.

Perceiving Our Bodies

Misuse of our bodies onstage is the amplified form of daily misuse. We thus have to begin with the self-awareness of everyday situations.

Everybody who speaks from experience of performance anxiety has throttled his body in some way or other. His body is not open enough, it is held tight, or it is too limp and thus blocked. Closed up. Since our bodies are creatures of habit, it doesn't help much if we delve into our mental first-aid kit at the last minute before a performance and pull out some kind of relaxation technique. At the very best, some kind of conditioning happens, a specific reaction occurring simultaneously with a perceived feeling—in this case, performance anxiety. With this affliction, it is a matter of much more than simply taking a tension and de-tensing it, as we could do with marionette strings. As opposed to a technique or an exercise which we always come up with when nervous, one which always serves the same ends and which we often practise, cold as a fish (the situation with most relaxation techniques), with performance anxiety we first of all have to become conscious of our bodies as such. This has nothing to do with well-known patterns of manipulation or control, but rather with the discovery of coming to ourselves. If we can experience our bodies as belonging to us, and not as a reaction to real or imagined judgments by others, then we can pull the rug out from underneath our anxiety. Then our own person can come through and express itself, our own perceivable reality will weigh more heavily than outside expectations, and we thus pave the way to power.

Why begin in everyday situations? Whenever we

appear in public, we bring ourselves into a situation which is challenging to our body and soul, one to which we respond with patterns belonging to our everyday repertoire. Onstage we do not present anything new, just whatever we are already familiar with, although perhaps in an excessive form. Misuse of our bodies onstage, in the last analysis, is nothing more than an amplified version of daily misuse. Thus we have to begin with the source of our dealings with our bodies: in our everyday lives.

Whoever wishes not merely to get rid of bothersome symptoms must begin at the beginning: that is, at the concrete self-awareness of the everyday monotony of habit. Such an approach has nothing to do with motoric activism or fitness training. On the contrary, it is a matter of finding our own movements associated with looseness, lightness, heaviness, and rhythm. It is also a matter of the way we succeed in this, but not by compulsive wishing or dogged practising. Finding our movements just seems to come by itself when we are inwardly at ease. If we learn to trust our own perceptions and to follow them, we will not only be capable of guiding our own movements by means of our bodily perception. We will also be in a position to imagine them in our inner eye, think them, and thus to practise them mentally. With all these bodily perceptions it is important that we feel at ease. Then all the functions of our brain will be better connected with one another, and all the parts of our bodies can participate in the learning experience.

If you are reading this book right now, leave off for a moment and take stock of how you are sitting. Is your back bent or straight? What about your shoulders, arms, and head? Your feet? How is your facial expression? Observe yourself inquisitively and collect your observations, for these will give you information on how you do what you do. Only then, when we know how we perform certain actions, are we able to change them. An entire method is based on this insight: the Alexander method, to which I will return later. Already the fact that we are capable of observing ourselves is the opposite pole to blind habit. It is altogether *the* prerequisite for changing old dysfunctional patterns and replacing them with new ones.

Now take this experience you have just had and transfer it to all the various activities of which your life is made up. Devote some time every day to your self-observation, take a break every now and then, and have a look at how your habits and patterns devolve. I don't mean just your bodily ones, but your mental and emotional customs as well. It is not a matter of reserving a set time each day for this activity, but rather to pause in the middle of your activities from time to time during the day. In this way we can find out much more about ourselves than if we were to set aside a special room, conveniently remote from our daily routine.

Observe how you stand, for example, when you are shopping or during a conversation. How is your weight distributed? Are you aware of your feet? At what angle do you like to hold your head? Observe yourself in a sitting position: do you distribute your weight more to the left or to the right? If you were to draw a picture of the way you look while sitting, how would it appear?

How do you move when you walk? How is your weight distributed? Is there a part of your body that leads? How does your gait change when you are tired, irritated, or happy? Do you have particular thought patterns while walking? What do you observe in other people when they pass by? How are your patterns of movement when climbing the stairs or bending over?

How is your voice when you speak? Even though it perhaps might seem strange to you, just go in front of a mirror and converse with yourself. Direct your attention to your mouth, your jaw, your chin, your eyes, and your head. What are your hands doing? And the rest of your body? Are there parts of your body that tense up while you are speaking? What sort of feelings and thoughts arise while you are observing yourself in the mirror?

Check your daily habits. How do you wake up, and what are your first perceptions? How do you move when getting out of bed? What is your spontaneous reaction when the telephone or doorbell rings?

Before we work on specific symptoms at all, we first have to get to know ourselves and develop our awareness. Without self-awareness, there is no self-change. This approach is to be distinguished from training programs forcing certain postures on us from outside, thus ignoring that our feeling of self-worth is based on self-awareness. In my opinion, this is also the reason why such training programs often fail. Instead of outside, we have to begin inside.

We will already have won the first battle when we stop moving mechanically, so as to perceive more consciously how we move through life. In so doing, we will discover our life patterns. Here I would like to introduce a new habit, one giving us the opportunity of becoming quiet, careful, and attentive, as children do when they are involved with their heart and soul in a matter. This new habit will let us find the bodily and spiritual repose allowing us to be 100% involved in what we are at a given moment. It is an exercise offering the possibility of deepened self-perception. I have adopted it from F. M. Alexander, the founder of the "Alexander Method": the habit of lying down on a daily basis, as a means of interrupting our daily activities. It is much simpler to become aware of ourselves in relation to the floor while lying down as opposed to standing up, a state in which we are only surrounded by air. The floor is like a neutral friend who allows us to recognize changes distinctly. Any time we expand our boundaries by means of new habits, this experience communicates itself by way of the respective nerve paths to our brain, where it becomes engraved. From then on it is also capable of being summoned up at any time. Therefore, we do not begin directly with the symptoms of performance anxiety, but first of all by taking pause, ceasing our daily hustle and bustle. In so doing we establish a counterpoint to our ingrained habits, thus giving our body the time and the opportunity to renew itself for freer functioning. In order to attain an optimal state of "collecting", we should reserve fifteen minutes a day for this exercise.

Collecting

Lie down on the floor on your back. Slip two or three books under your head, so that your spine is lying flat on the floor and is no longer curved. Take time to arrive. Lay your hands loosely on your abdomen and bend your knees. Remain in this position for at least 15 minutes, breathing in and out in a completely natural way. You will be surprised how fresh and energy-laden you will find yourself after this exercise. This lying-down exercise interrupts the daily routine of our incorrect use of the body. Our body can straighten itself again and attain its balance, and our breathing will become freer and more open.

Patterns of Movement Are Patterns of Life

If we can succeed in relaxing the muscles of our body, then our mental state will also become relaxed.

Bodily symptoms of performance anxiety can be coped with if we occupy ourselves with the kinesthetic perception of our body: that is, by sensing our muscles, tendons, and joints—our perception of movement. Not until we have gained access to our perceptions of movement can we influence them systematically. To make clear what I mean by kinesthetic perception, let us begin with a simple experiment:

> Close your eyes.
> Lift one of your arms very slowly towards the ceiling, until it is pointing straight up.
> In so doing, follow every perception which arises...

It is our kinesthetic sense to which we owe being able to perform this exercise with our eyes closed. It is not necessary for us to see what we are doing; we can trust our kinesthetic sense, which provides for coordination, direction, and well-being. To deepen our feeling for the body, let me now suggest a few basic perception exercises, a few systematic exercises for particular symptoms, as well as possibilities for a quick relax just before a performance.

Studying Your Body

> Lie down on your back on a surface which is not too soft. Your arms should be extended to the sides next

to your body, palms down; your legs are slightly opened.

Close your eyes and allow silence to set in.

Feel the contact of the underside of your body with the floor.

Direct your attention to your left foot, your toes, your heel, the ball of your foot, and your ankle.

Now change over to the right foot, and observe it in the same way.

Allow your perception to wander over to your left leg, knee, thigh, and hip, and then to your right leg. Just observe, as if you were to be "listening" to your legs without trying to "put them straight".

Allow ideas, pictures, and feelings to appear. You will be able to find out more about your legs if you enter into a dialogue with their various parts; for example, "Knee, what message do you have for me?"

Now direct your attention to your arms, and compare them with one another. Try to locate their differences and to formulate them to yourself.

Go into your fingers, hands, wrists, forearms, elbows, upper arms, shoulders, and all the way up to your head. Notice how it is lying, how your scalp feels. Continue your wandering to your ears, forehead, and eyelids. Observe if you feel any tension there. Continue to your eyes, nose, cheeks, and lips, and to the inside of your mouth, to teeth and tongue. Reconnoiter the inside of your mouth, the upper and lower arching and the cavity between.

Notice your breathing, where the air enters and streams out again. Feel how your breath causes your neck, back, and chest to rise and fall.

Speak with the individual parts of your body that

attract your attention, and allow yourself to be guided by ideas and images.

Direct your attention towards the areas of your rib cage, ribs, and down into your pelvis. Investigate your pelvic area, go into your buttocks and from there into your back.

Just go along your spine a few times—from your pelvis to the edge of your skull. Can you determine if the relation of your spine to the floor changes when you inhale or exhale?

Now go a little farther with your perception, into your center located underneath the navel —your hara— and from there try to establish contact to your stomach, your liver, and your intestines, and try to make them come into a dialogue with you.

Take as much time for this trip as you need. It is worthwhile to follow your manifold observations as slowly and carefully as possible, lingering here or there as necessary. You are not obliged to follow the route I suggest, but observe yourself thereby. Where do you like to spend more time, where not? Which parts do you pass over?

Muscle Tension

We all know that our feeling of well-being requires good muscle tonus. What does this mean: "good muscle tonus"? Take the trim athletes and the purposeful joggers who, as we know now, will suffer from detrition in later life. In the face of this information is it not more sensible to stay away from body-building and fitness centers and rather to meditate instead? The answers to such questions are confusing, just as with the subject of nutrition. For this reason, I prefer to appeal to common sense, and my opinion is: maximum results with minimal muscular effort. Good muscle tonus, then, means just as much tension as necessary for a particular action, neither more nor less. The opposite, or unsuitable muscular effort, therefore implies too little or too much tension.

With performance anxiety, we generally have too much muscular tension in our bodies. Fear causes our muscles to contract, and this shows how our thoughts can influence our body in a deep and powerful way. However, the opposite is also true: our muscular tension can influence our thinking. Therefore, if we think that we are tensed up, our muscles react by contracting still more; and if, for example, we imagine that our neck muscles are slowly loosening up, then they will feel themselves addressed and gradually will relax—a most important fact for our discussion of performance power. That is, if we can succeed in relaxing the muscles of our body, then our mental state will become de-tensed, and we will feel ourselves calmer and freer. Athletes are used to thoughts of this kind, as opposed for instance to musicians, who have hardly occupied themselves at all with matters like this up to now. We can learn from star athletes how to influence our body via our psyche. I have utilized their knowledge to put together a few suggestions which will be of use to people in many diverse performing situations:

Releasing

Most people today find themselves in a constant state of tension, and many of them do not even notice any more how tense they are. Thus they are not even in a position to compensate for such a state by themselves. In the last analysis, performance anxiety is nothing but an intensification of the vicious circle "tension—cramping up". In dealing with this state, first of all we should leave the well-trodden path and allow our surplus tensions to escape. In so doing, we are letting go; that is, we release ourselves from something, let it be, or let it escape. However, this also necessitates our releasing ourselves from our active will, simply allowing bodily blocks and blockades to dissolve.

> Sit upright on a stool or chair and place your hands palms up on your thighs. Your back should be straight.
>
> Close your eyes and center your head by allowing it to move to and fro in all directions until it is completely free of any tension.
>
> Hearken inwards to your breathing and simply let it come and go without trying to influence it in any way.
>
> Experience how your muscles become tired and how you sink into a feeling of warmth and heaviness. Remain this way and allow whatever comes to happen.
>
> After awhile come out of your state of relaxation by breathing deeply and by tensing and relaxing your muscles a few times, as well as yawning with zest.
>
> Your limbs are now light and mobile. You feel wide awake and open your eyes.

Becoming Calm and Composed

> Lie down on the floor on a mat or thick rug, on your back. Your arms are lying next to your body palms down, your legs are opened slightly, and your toes are pointing out.
>
> Close your eyes and allow silence to prevail.
>
> Imagine that your body is a sponge filled with water, lying on the floor, and inspired by the sole wish of

releasing the water from all its pores.
In your thoughts, open the pores of the soles of your feet; let the water escape and finally evaporate.
With this inner image, wander through all the various parts of your body: legs, pelvic area, chest cavity, along your ribs into your arms, your hands, and up to your head. You can assist the water's escape by imagining yourself to breathe quickly and deeply in and out several times through the bodily part in question.

If now you hearken inside yourself, you will experience how your sternum sinks lower and lower with every breath. You feel very light and relaxed.

Now envision your impending performance. While your inner vision becomes ever clearer, repeat to yourself the following words: "I see myself in a state of total release and completely alert." Let your performance transpire like an inner video, follow every detail, and repeat: "I am completely relaxed and alert."

Becoming Still Calmer

With the next imagination exercise you will see what it means to be still more calm and composed:

With your eyes closed, imagine you were a rubber doll, your limbs connected not with joints, but with rubber bands.
Now try to move your body with its rubber limbs like a snake; and in so doing, enjoy how supple everything feels.

167

> Let yourself go completely, merge into a feeling of heaviness.
> Enjoy this heaviness and calmness to the full.
> After this, rest a bit and investigate how warm and pliant you feel.
> Come out of your state of relaxation by deep breathing in and out, by stretching your arms and legs, tensing and releasing all your muscles. Open your eyes, yawn, and stretch some more.

With these various possibilities of relaxation, we now possess an essential tool for reducing disturbing symptoms of tension. Besides the muscular relaxation reaction, which has a settling influence on the fight-or-flight reaction encountered with performance anxiety, we can also reduce the activity of our brain waves. We can see and think more clearly again. Furthermore, our body temperature rises; this is particularly important for those suffering from cold hands. Already at the first try, you will feel a transformation of the energy level of the various parts of your body into which you "breathe".

Muscular Relaxation

In conclusion, an all-embracing relaxation exercise. This one is particularly effective before one enters the limelight because of its use of inner images.[44]

> Lie down on the floor in the Alexander position described above. Become silent and hearken inwards.
> Imagine that your body is a lake. It is raining onto this lake. The raindrops disturbing the surface of the lake

are your thoughts.

Envision how the rain slowly ceases to fall; the raindrops become fewer just as your thoughts calm down and become silent.

When your thoughts have come to rest, it is now time to allow your body to relax. Start with your head and neck. Tell yourself that all your neck muscles are relaxed and in balance.

Speak in this way to all the parts of your head. A few suggestions for so doing: "My eyes are relaxed inside and outside, and my eyelids are resting peacefully on my eyeballs. My jaw is loose and relaxed. My forehead, my eyebrows, and my nose are soft and relaxed."

Picture to yourself how all the parts of your head become relaxed. Think of how you relax your mouth even into the depths of your throat, and how you expand your neck and throat muscles slightly, thus loosening them.

Tell yourself: "Now my neck is relaxed."

Concentrate on the word "relaxed" while your thoughts wander slowly down your spine, all the way to your coccyx. Picture how each individual vertebra increases in size, as if all of them were to soak up bodily fluids like sponges, and imagine how your pelvis and buttocks become soft and relaxed.

Let your attention wander in every direction over your entire back and from it outwards to the room you are lying in.

While your back is expanding widely, your chest cavity opens up. Your shoulders release their tension at the same time that you visualize how all the muscles between your neck and shoulders relax, expanding slightly.

View in your mind's eye how your armpit muscles loosen, thus freeing up room for breathing and blood circulation.

Wander into your arms and hands, visualize the muscles of your elbow, your wrists, and your finger joints and how they gently relax.

Finally, direct your attention to your legs and hips. All the muscles of your hip region become released and free, and this relaxation continues on into your legs.

An useful aid to imagination is a triangle. Both your legs form the two upright sides of the triangle, while your back and feet form its base. Now picture to yourself how both sides of the triangle are pulled upwards by a gentle pull of your knees, thus expanding and relaxing the muscles in your hips, ankles, and legs.

We can develop further ideas for relaxation ourselves. In so doing, it is important that that part of us doing the observing constantly remains alert, sending back word of new perceptions of expansion and relaxation. When you have ended this muscular relaxation exercise and slowly stand up again, you will notice interesting changes within your body. The more time you take for yourself, the more elasticity you will attain and the better your feeling of well-being.

Spinal Relaxation

The two following possibilities are particularly useful if we want to zero in on certain specific symptoms. Whoever can say of himself, "I have a certain feeling at the back of my neck", is well served by the following exercise, the goal of which is freeing up blockades in the spine.[45]

Lie down on your back and slide small pillows under your neck and knees. Your arms should be lying loosely next to your body, your legs are opened slightly, and your toes are pointing outwards.

With your eyes open, stare at a fixed spot on the ceiling. Close them after awhile.

Slowly start to move to and fro with small lolling motions, starting with your head, neck, shoulders, arms, hands, and back.

Be attentive that your spine comes to lie gently and loosely on the floor.

Then move your buttocks and pelvic area in the same loose manner, also your legs and feet. Check your observations, and then rest a moment.

Now in your thoughts go down your spine, vertebra for vertebra, starting in the neck area. Then the chest area, finally the back area.

Notice where the blockades are and loosen them by "breathing" several times deeply into the respective areas.

Now while inhaling and without otherwise moving your legs, tense the muscles of your upper foot in such a way that your toes are pulled upwards and towards the middle of your body, at the same time tensing your buttock muscles forcefully; on exhaling, let go first your buttocks, then your toes. Repeat this procedure at least three times.

Now while you inhale deeply, push your chin into your chest, your elbows in an outward direction, and your hands, angled off, upwards; release while exhaling.

Repeat three times.

Now try the whole procedure as a mental exercise. Mental practice, or visualizing, is an important tool, since in front of an audience we usually cannot interrupt our activity in order to do calisthenics. We are thus left to the device of mentally summoning up certain bodily sensations which are not outwardly visible.

Mentally place yourself in the position of your spine. Through visualization, on inhaling pull your toes and hands upwards, angle your arms outwards, and tense up your buttocks and shoulders; on exhaling, release these areas slowly, with a liberating feeling.

After a short break roll over onto your stomach, "breathe" deeply into your back several times, simultaneously pulling your shoulders up.

Then loosen your body with small shaking movements, starting with your head and finishing with your feet. When you feel yourself to be completely relaxed, turn over onto your back and rest awhile.

Notice how warm and supple your back feels, and enjoy the feeling of well-being emanating from your relaxed back.

Hand, Wrist, and Arm Relaxation

With the following exercise I am thinking particularly of those musicians who play keyboard instruments, as well as those others whose activity depends mainly on their elbows and wrists being relaxed. Blocks in one's shoulders, arms, and hands can be released by this exercise, which opens up the energy channels of the upper body.

This relaxation exercise can be performed in a sitting, standing, or reclining position.

Shake your head, your limbs, and your body loosely for awhile. The smaller the movements, the greater the relaxation effect.

Now start to relax your joints. Roll your head slowly from its central position to the left and back, then to the right and back. In so doing, see that your breathing is completely free and relaxed. Repeat this rolling at least ten times.

Now on inhaling clench your fists tightly, and on exhaling release them. Repeat several times.

Then allow your forearms to swing forward and back with a pendulous motion. Do the same with your entire arms until your shoulder joints glide forward and back completely freely.

Next, with circular motions, move both shoulder joints several times from front to back. Take a short break.

Resume the loose pendulous motions of your forearms, back and forth; allow your wrists to circulate gently, snake-like, and then to make swan-like motions back and forth.

In performing this exercise, it is important that you incorporate your breathing rhythmically into all your various patterns of movement; this way the releasing effect will be significantly increased.

As a conclusion, tense all the muscles of your body and then release them; stretch all over, breathing deeply in and out at the same time.

A Quiet Place

The relaxation exercise which follows is at the same time an excellent one for visualizing. It is also based on the principle that relaxed muscles create a feeling of well-being in the psyche. For those people who like to use their imagination, it is the ideal way of "flowing". This method has a particular advantage: it is fast. With enough practice it takes effect immediately—an ideal possibility just before going onstage or in a short break. It was made known by John Syer and Chris Connolly of the Sporting Bodymind Organization under the title of "The quiet place".[46]

Sit or lie down in a place where you cannot be disturbed.

Close your eyes and take a few deep breaths.

Visualize yourself in one of your favorite places—an oasis of peace and restfulness —at the seaside, in the mountains, or in the woods. Any place that is your place, where you feel peaceful and relaxed.

Look around the place in your mind's eye, and take in its every element—the sounds, odors, colors. Plunge still deeper into your experiencing of the place. What is so particular about it? What makes it so peaceful? Enjoy the feeling of peace and relaxation to the full. Allow yourself to drift like a cloud in the wind, and enjoy this wonderful feeling of infinite lightness.

Now without opening your eyes, bring your attention back to the room in which you find yourself, and squeeze your right thumb with the fingers of your left hand. In so doing, go back once again to your place and visualize all the details.

Repeat this procedure by letting the scene fade away, then squeeze your thumb again and return to the quiet place.

Repeat this procedure three times in all before letting go of your thumb for good and opening your eyes.

With this technique, you will have set an "anchor" capable of being summoned up at any time. After a few tries it will already suffice just to squeeze your thumb: this alone will be enough to bring you back to your place whenever you want, whenever you feel the need for relaxation.

Breathing

To be able to perceive ourselves in our breathing is a prerequisite for influencing our performance power by our breathing.

Now that we have occupied ourselves with muscle relaxation, it is obvious that we should now deal with our most important and most natural muscle movement: our breathing. No matter what method of relaxation you have chosen up to now, breathing is a fundamental part of this process. As the most important mediator between body, mind, and soul, our breathing exerts a profound and direct influence on all the areas of our existence. It reflects to us how we live, and not only does it mirror inner processes both intellectual and emotional, but it also stimulates them.

When we are afflicted with performance anxiety, our breathing rhythm is also disturbed, and our breathing is shallow, agitated, and irregular. If we are able to settle our breathing down so that it becomes steady, calm, and slow, all of the symptoms mentioned above will be affected. Our bodies will be more relaxed, our thoughts clearer, and our feelings assuaged.

To be able to perceive ourselves in our breathing and thus in our own body is the main prerequisite for influencing our performance power by way of our breathing. To be aware of ourselves in our breathing is at the same time an effective method of relaxing. That is, just as we concentrate our attention onto our breathing, we will automatically become less tense and more at ease. I have taken over a few systematic suggestions in this area from Ilse Middendorf's teachings about breathing, which she developed in her work in Berlin with singers and actors:[47]

1. Observing Our Breathing

Press the tip of your tongue onto that part of your palate located directly in front of the uvula, let your tongue be relaxed.

Remain this way for the duration of about ten breaths.

Notice where it is that your breath moves, and whether you feel yourself to be calmer...

2. A Mental Walk

Go for a little mental walk with me.

Summon up your imagination and allow your breathing to come by itself:

- Visualize that you are walking over a meadow of delicate, fresh grass. The sun is shining. You are enjoying its warmth—where is your breath moving, and of what do you become aware?

- You are walking through warm, soft, dry sand—how does your breathing react?

- You descend into the bed of a brook, the water comes up to your knees, and you walk through to the other side—where is the motion of your breathing?

- You continue and cross over a concrete platform—where do you feel your breathing now?

- You end your little stroll on a freshly plowed field, the earth is soft and moist, and your feet are sinking down—where is your breath now?

Another simple exercise that causes tensions to be released by bringing us into the middle of our body is the following one:

3. Exhaling for Inhaling

Be aware of your breathing while standing in a position which is as free and loose as possible, let your breath be expelled a few times with a sigh, and wait for the next inhalation; it will come all by itself.

Then lengthen your exhalations little by little, slightly more each time.

Observe how your inhalations respond to this. You will notice: the longer the exhalation, the more intensive the following inhalation.

If you continue to intensify this fluctuation, your exhalation will become long and regular, and your inhalation will deepen.

This kind of awareness of our breathing will effect a decided loosening of bodily tensions if we succeed in letting the air flow by itself instead of drawing it in forcefully. Among musicians, it is mostly singers and wind players who have difficulties allowing it to flow, since professionally they are required to do so much with their breathing. The first thing they have to learn is to do nothing, just let it come.

Breathing Exercises are Exhalation Exercises

An essential goal of any work on breathing is finding our own natural breathing rhythm. Breathing should be allowed to happen, not drilled. An important principle is: breathing exercises are exhalation exercises. Thus, channeled exhaling is the watchword. As opposed to what has often been written about the supposedly relaxing effect of deep inhalation, I would like to offer my own observation that deep inhalations rather tend to tighten the throat and neck.

Here I would like to suggest two very effective breathing exercises which you should always have in readiness in your spiritual first-aid kit before performances. Both of them will have a beneficial braking effect if you employ them at the first signs of performance anxiety:

1. Basic Breathing

The first exercise consists in exhaling slowly and calmly through your nose. This will deepen your inhalation and give you a deepened awareness of your inhalation.

You can use this simple method whenever you feel yourself in danger of losing your inner balance. Not only does it release tensions, but it can also help you build up new tonus when you feel limp.

178

If you perspire heavily, have moist hands, or if your voice often trembles from excitement, the second exercise can be of valuable help. It belongs to actors' and public speakers' basic equipment:

2. Speakers' Friend

While sitting or standing, tense up your stomach muscles as if you were pulling them in tightly with a corset, and still better with your hands stretched straight forward, your bent elbows pressed into your sides. With your mouth slightly opened, breathe out with a noticeable hissing sound.

At the end of the phase of exhalation, allow your stomach muscles and your arms to relax, and let the air flow in gently.

Always use this exercise when you feel performance anxiety coming on. It should be part of your basic bag of tricks. Tensing up your stomach muscles prevents fear-producing substances such as noradrenaline or epinephrine (adrenaline) from being set free in your body. The effect is: you automatically become calmer. In addition, your diaphragm muscles become activated, whereby the air reaches your vocal cords with more pressure, and your voice will project better.

Breathing in Five Parts

The breathing exercise which follows here, breathing in five parts, is a mild form of self-hypnosis which relieves bodily tensions and clears up confusion of thoughts. After a bit of practice with this method it is possible to relax very quickly, and this method will also prove to be effective in highly challenging, stressful situations.[49]

> Lie down or sit comfortably, close your eyes, both arms at your sides.
>
> Inhale deeply. Concentrate on relaxing your face and neck muscles while exhaling.
>
> Take a second deep breath. While exhaling, allow the muscles in your arms and shoulders to loosen.
>
> Take a third deep breath. This time when you exhale, relax the muscles of your rib cage, stomach, and back.
>
> Take a fourth deep breath. Now the muscles in your legs and feet become relaxed during exhalation.
>
> Now inhale deeply for the fifth time and concentrate your attention on relaxing your entire body while you breathe out. Remain in this attitude of relaxation as long as you like.
>
> If you want to be fully present again, then count down slowly from 5 to 1; in so doing, tell yourself that you will find yourself as relaxed and wide awake as you wish to be for the task ahead.
>
> You will keep this feeling when your consciousness is completely in the present once again.

Hara—in Unison with Gravity

Awareness of our abdominal area relieves our worn-out nerves. Its effect is that of a fortress in the surf of performance anxiety.

In this day and age of stress and competition, it is instructive to observe that concepts of the "middle of the body" are receiving increasing attention. For anyone suffering from performance anxiety, one subject is of key importance: feeling centered in the middle of our bodies, being "in *hara*", as the Japanese say. After all, to be afflicted with performance anxiety means precisely the opposite: to be out of balance, topheavy, uncentered. Therefore we must deal with the way we can find our center, our hara; from that point we can look for ways to retain the feeling of being rooted there, so as to utilize it for our actions.

Now the question is: how can we find our center, that point where our energy is centered? Traditionally this center is located between one and four inches (3-10 cm) under the navel. There is a simple method of determining for ourselves exactly where this point lies:

Cough forcefully into your abdominal region, and with the palm of your hand search for the point where your abdomen thrusts forward most noticeably. There your personal hara is located, the point of your greatest stability and security.

Concentrate on this spot, place your inhaled air right there, and you will notice that you feel more resolute and firm.

You can also test this feeling: while you are centered in hara, let someone else push at you. He will notice a strong natural resistance.

However, if you fix your attention upon your highest point, your forehead, you will experience the exact opposite: extreme instability and insecurity. From this we can deduce that the more topheavy we are, the easier it is to put us out of balance; but the more we are centered in our abdomen, the more stability we will gain.

It is not without reason that for the Japanese, a person out of hara is an unstable person. If we can find our center and collect ourselves there by sending our breathing into that area, then we will have stability and power. We will be completely at one with ourselves, absolutely in the here and now. This feeling of "being here" is the best medicine against fear and performance anxiety. That is, when we are fully in the present, fear cannot get at us, for our fear is always projected into the future.

Directing our energy into our hara brings us into contact with another natural law: gravity. Without gravity, our movements are unthinkable. On the one hand it is a matter of maintaining our erect posture against gravity, and on the other, of how we go along with gravity, reacting in agreement with it. Performance anxiety is always associated with the fact that we do not entrust ourselves to the force of gravity, thereby losing our natural balance. We thus become light and topheavy, instead of centering ourselves in the lower regions of our body where our weight lies. We will be able to arrive at a feeling for our own weight if we don't pull our weight upwards, whereby too much blood would be collected in the upper half of our body, but rather transfer it downwards, allowing ourselves to feel our weight coming from below.

Where we carry our weight cannot only be seen, it can also be heard. We will appear insecure and strained, and our voice will sound unsupported, if we pull our weight too far upwards, and vice versa: if we give our weight over to the force of gravity, we will be fully aware, and our voice will have resonance. As an example of this, a well-known violinist once heard a live recording of a colleague and remarked, "He's standing on his tiptoes while he plays." This proves that our distribution of weight has a noticeable effect on the way we perform—and it is certain that music-making is not the only area affected. In this connection I would like to mention a commonly observed phenomenon, especially with pianists: raised or drawn-up shoulders. This posture is not only unnatural; it also leads to a separation within the body between the upper half which is pulled upwards and the lower half which gravitates downwards.

The principle of gravity becomes evident if we visualize ourselves lifting a heavy object. If we do not support the weight from below, it is first of all very strenuous and second, it is downright dangerous: we could lift ourselves out of joint. Therefore, it corresponds to a natural law that we center our weight in the lower half of our body. This gives us strength and footing, as well as weight in the full sense of the word, lending our body a natural feeling of balance.

To illuminate this principle, I would like to make an observation about our speech. That some people are listened to more than others also has to do with the principle of gravity. Indeed, this usually has nothing to do with what is said, but how it is said: it is a matter of the quality and the "weight" behind the spoken word. In other words, the weight or quality behind our words determines whether we will be listened to or not, and in what way. The better we are centered in the lower half of our body, the more quality, resonance, and depth our voice will have. Now we can understand why it is that we have difficulty listening to public speakers with high, shallow, thin voices: we are missing their weight, the depth of their presence.

The process of becoming centered in the lower half of our body takes time. We are too used to living in our heads, our thoughts, our spines—our fortresses against a threatening world. Hara awareness relieves our worn-out nerves and our head. Its effect is that of a fortress in the surf of performance anxiety.

The exercises following now are meant to show us ways of gaining and retaining a connection with our center. We will first begin with the technique of "centering". Here it is a matter of focussing our attention on our hara. Centering ourselves in the middle of our body has a calming and regulative effect to which we can also take recourse in moments of extreme performance anxiety. With sufficient practice, a feeling of relaxation and control can appear after only a few seconds.

Centering

Stand up straight, with your arms hanging loosely at your sides.

Close your eyes and breathe calmly and regularly.

While inhaling, perceive how the tension in the upper part of your body increases, whereas with exhalation you have a feeling of heaviness and sinking down.

While you breathe in, notice the tension in your face, neck, and shoulders. While you breathe out, allow these tensions to glide away from you; concentrate on the feeling of heaviness in your abdominal area.

Continue to breathe calmly and regularly, and while doing so, direct your attention inwards to your hara. Keep your attention there and go on breathing normally; you will feel completely safe and calm.

Hara Breathing

To develop more feeling for your personal hara, I suggest hara breathing.

Lay your hands on your abdomen and inhale slowly, until you are pleasantly filled up with air. Wait a moment and then exhale with the help of a long-drawn-out "ffff" from your half-opened mouth.

During exhalation, allow your imagination to develop the feeling of being freed from a heavy weight, and say to yourself: "I am as steady and invulnerable as a rock."

The Lake[50]

The next exercise combines breathing and visualization to an all-embracing feeling of being centered.

Sit down on a chair, lay your hands on the area of your hara and direct your attention there.

Feel how your body expands from this center in all directions.

Hearken to your breathing, and imagine how it enters your body like fog, there being transformed into a liquid flowing into your hara. Your hara is a lake, and with every breath it becomes more and more filled up.

Feel this "lake" with your hands and enjoy to the full the feeling of being safe in it and being carried by it.

Inside and Outside

With this pleasant feeling of being centered in hara, let us proceed one step further. Now we will try to retain this feeling while moving about and directing our attention to our environment.

Your hands remain on the area of your hara.

Look around, and with your attention always wander back to your center of energy.

Stand up and walk around.

Check from time to time if you are still centered in your hara.

Go for a walk with this feeling of being centered, and allow your attention continually to wander back and forth between your interior place and the environment outside.

Your ability to concentrate doubly, inside and outside, will be heightened still more if you go among people. Play with the feeling; that is, simply observe if you lose your center or if you succeed effortlessly in remaining centered. The more self-evident your double observation becomes, the easier it will be for you to become centered and to retain the feeling of being centered while onstage.

Being Grounded

Closely tied up with the concept of being centered is that of grounding; that is, a person's contact with the earth, with his own reality. The extent of our self-confidence depends on how we succeed in grounding ourselves. Well grounded, we feel ourselves to be secure on our legs, we have our feet on the floor, we know who we are and where we stand at the moment, and our movements are light and graceful. People who are not grounded enough are in danger of becoming overwhelmed by strong feelings or perceptions. Fearful of this, they throttle their perceptions— a state which can often be recognized in that they lock their knees, causing their legs to be stiff and without feeling.

With performance anxiety, too, we are in danger of losing the ground under our feet. Our feeling of conviction and security shrinks, and we tense our legs; our contact with the ground is, so to speak, purely mechanical. Now, if we can succeed in regaining a good contact with the earth, our feeling of security will increase and we will feel our power coming into us. Often enough, simply relaxing our leg muscles will suffice, and we then feel with relief that we don't have to exert ourselves unduly but should just surrender ourselves confidently to Mother Earth. Sometimes in crisis situations or before important events it will be necessary to become grounded again, so as to find our feeling of balance and inner security. For myself, I have discovered a tried and true "house recipe" for becoming grounded: I go into the woods and embrace a tree—a strong, healthy tree. However, not everybody is living in the country, and so I would like to offer some other possibilities guaranteeing a good feeling of being grounded.

The following exercise, a standard one for grounding, derives from bioenergetic therapy after Alexander Lowen.[51] It has a deeply relaxing effect and should be done not only before performances, but also ought to belong to our daily morning ritual, just like brushing our teeth.

Grounding

Your feet are placed parallel to each other, about one and a half feet apart (50 cm).
Slowly lean over forwards with your upper body, so that the fingertips of both hands touch the ground. Your head is hanging down completely loosely, and

your knees are bent as much as necessary. Your body is resting on the balls of your feet, not on your fingertips or heels.

Leaving your fingertips in contact with the ground, straighten your knees slowly, however without locking them or making them completely straight or stiff. Feel how your coccyx moves upwards.

Hold this position for about 25 breaths, breathing effortlessly and deeply.

If your legs should begin to vibrate, this means that the energy flow is slowly starting to function.

If you don't feel any vibration in your legs, this probably means that you have tensed them too much. In such a case, bend them again, and then push them slightly backwards once more.

Repeat the entire process a few times, so that your muscles can become relaxed. However, don't bend or stretch your knees more than necessary—just enough that they still feel supple.

Practise this exercise for the duration of at least 25 breaths until the vibration begins. You will notice your breathing become deeper and more spontaneous.

When you regain your normal standing position, see to it that your knees are slightly bent, your feet are parallel to one another, and your weight tends in a forward direction. If your legs should still vibrate a little, this speaks for the exercise's invigorating effect.

Finally, here is one of the simplest and most pleasurable possibilities of grounding: do something that you enjoy! This can be playing ping-pong, swimming, going for a walk, or taking an effervescent bubble bath.

Sometimes even a piece of cake or a cup of coffee can work wonders—despite all information to the contrary!

10

Integration Work

Power performance requires integration work. This will reconcile our emotions, our conflicts, and our self-perception with one another.

If we try for performance power by working exclusively on the corporeal level, forgetting that we as human beings also have a spiritual dimension, our effectivity will be just as reduced as if we were to work only on the psychic level. The various dimensions of performance anxiety—in body, soul, and mind—are in fact interrelated, implying each other and affecting each other reciprocally. A person whose inner balance is affected by performance anxiety can thus count on being affected in all of these areas together. To be sure, it cannot always be determined on which level the primary, causative disturbance lies. Perhaps that is not so important. What for me is essential is to recognize the indissoluble bonds with which everything affects everything else.

Performance anxiety is always determined by disintegrative tendencies, ones which are not tuned to each other. Our body is exhausted, but our mind is wide awake: feelings and thoughts are vying with one other, thoughts are quarreling with perceptions. How can we get out of this vicious circle in which these various areas are clashing with one another? How can we come to fine tuning or integration, so that body, soul, and mind work as one?

In the preceding chapter, we approached performance power mainly on the bodily level. Now the subjective aspect of our thoughts and feelings shall be addressed. It is answers to questions concerning these aspects that I have placed under the heading "Integration Work". In this chapter I would like to show ways of learning to understand our emotions, inner conflicts, and our bodily and self-perception better, so as to integrate them.

Let me present three aids to integration which, to be sure, have been known for centuries but in our time have often been ignored.

The first one is guided imagination, the training of our mind's eye through *visualization*. Anyone experimenting with this will learn to investigate the dynamics of his own performance anxiety.

A second aid, related to the first, is *affirmation*. With this, we can consciously change unconscious attitudes and influence the activity of our brain waves.

The third one with which we will occupy ourselves is called by scholars "relaxation reaction", a kind of *alert relaxation* exerting a soothing effect on our conflict-oriented inner voices.

These aids are mere tools which require neither special skills nor long, arduous experience. I have personally tested their efficacy on my clients and on myself. These aids, taken alone or combined, have furnished the key to changes in personality and intuitive insights. I am sure that you, too, can profit from these resources, on the way to your own personal performance power.

Visualization

If we recognize how certain mental images can influence us, then we can influence this process ourselves by a systematic employment of mental images and visualization techniques.

Guided imagination—or visualization, as it is also called—belongs to the most efficient strategies in coping with performance anxiety and thus developing performance power. Those people who suffer from performance anxiety have got used to dealing with mental images that continually devolve before their mind's eye like movies about catastrophes. Just as our inner voices can sabotage us, so do our mental images. We all are familiar with wishful thinking and nightmares and how they can become so vivid within us that they exert a real influence on our lives. They can cause our thoughts to have wings, or conversely, they can block us completely.

Emile Coué once said: "If the will and the power of imagination are battling for control, it will always be the imagination that wins."[52] This means that if we spurn our imagination onwards and direct it with our will-power, beliefs, and expectations, and simultaneously school ourselves to make our goals come to life in such a way that we can see, feel, hear, smell, and touch them, then we will also be able to accomplish what we set out to do. We will be able to change our mental images—instead of the feared catastrophe we can envision the nicest possibility—and also change the ways in which we imagine. For example, many people are strongly motivated if they imagine something as being very colorful or extremely large. Others react strongly to the tone of their inner voices which either give them wings or are inhibiting. Just as a movie director can change the effect his film has on his audience, we can change the effect that experiences exert on us. If we have come to recognize the various ways in which particular mental images influence us, then we can start to exercise control over them by a systematic employment of specific visualization techniques.

The constructive utilization of our own power of imagination requires more than unstructured day-dreaming. If our goal is to summon up experiences or construct them anew, we will have to learn to channel and consciously guide our imagination. If we thus systematically put our imagination into action, it can work in two ways. First, we will be able to draw images and messages out of our unconscious, thus summoning up inner knowledge, or second, we will be able to transport messages from the sphere of our consciousness into deeper levels of our unconscious.

Although "imagination" normally implies dealing with inner images, there are actually various possibilities of introducing our power of phantasy. The reason for this is that people have different approaches to their sensory channels, using them in different ways. Many communicate with their brain above all in a visual frame of reference: they react mainly to the images they see. There are others who are primarily auditive; that is, they react particularly strongly to what they hear. Still others have a kinesthetic disposition, reacting mainly to things they can touch. If we have found out that we tend to be motivated visually, auditively, or kinesthetically, we can employ this knowledge to motivate ourselves and to act efficiently in various situations. Some people get worried because they are unable to *see* a mental picture. This worry is completely unfounded, for it is just as good if we can feel, smell, hear, or grasp. Therefore, it is not at all necessary actually to see a clear picture in front of our inner eye. Instead, it is a matter of developing that kind of imagination proper to us alone, and using it in the most lively possible way.

A further aspect has recently come increasingly to public attention: the orientation of our inner images. It is necessary to differentiate between inner and outer perception. Inner perception has to do with the view of what is going on around us, in such a way as if we were actually to perform a certain activity ourselves. Our perception, so to speak, takes place in the first person singular and comprises everything we see and feel from our point of view. Conversely, with outer perception we observes ourselves from outside as through a camera; we see ourselves, so to speak, in the third person. Physiologically, each of these two forms of perception has a different effect. The "first-person perception" leads to more intensive muscular activity and is therefore more effective for motor skills in athletics or music than "third-person perception".[53] Although this is the most commonly used method, it seems important to me that we utilize our knowledge of the effectivity of inner perception in dealing with performance anxiety.

Let me now summarize the various possibilities offered by the power of our imagination:
- Inner perception: I see myself.
- Outer perception: I observe myself from outside.
- Kinesthetic perception: I imagine the feeling I have while performing a certain activity; for example, I imagine how I go onstage, bow, and accept the applause, how I stand up and walk over to the speaker's lectern, or how I run onto the field and wave to the spectators.
- Auditive perception: I can hear myself, for example, speaking loudly and clearly to my audience.

We will best utilize our power of imagination if it includes a comprehensive sensory awareness coming from all our possible senses. It is evident that we will profit more from our inside world if we can feed it or tap it through various channels simultaneously. In fact, the difference between what is going on in our imagination and what really happens is much smaller than we generally assume. Experiments have shown that if we imagine a particular activity to ourselves, the muscles responsible for such an activity register tiny electric impulses similar to those registered when we actually perform the activity. Our brain works deductively; therefore, the production of an idea tends to cause our brain to act as though the idea were reality.

Imagination and the Alpha State

Our imagination plays a valuable and integrative role in bridging the gap between the conscious and the unconscious, between the rational and affective dimensions of performance anxiety. However, the power of our imagination can only come into play if we are in a relaxed state of readiness for reception; that is, in a state in which our brain waves vibrate on the so-called alpha frequency. Neurologists are in agreement that the alpha state is the best one for learning. In such a state we are both alert and fully relaxed. Furthermore, it is fun to learn in this condition, because it refreshes and regenerates us. If an excess of brain-wave activity is the root of performance anxiety, then we can deduce from this that it would contribute to a solution of our problem if we could learn to guide our brain-wave activity. When we are in an alpha state, our brain-wave frequency lies between 7 and 14 cycles per second (cps), a condition we experience while daydreaming or shortly before falling asleep. In a normal waking state, when we emit beta waves, our brain-waves vibrate between 15 and 21 cps, thus considerably faster. Under the pressure of performance anxiety the frequency is generally from 22 to 25 cps or even more, depending on the individual fear level. At this frequency there is no more concentration, and our thoughts go out of control.

If we wish to gain access to our inner resources, then, we must first learn to relax ourselves consciously to the alpha level, thus reducing the activity of our brain waves. This is a condition which can appear in any meditation or fervent prayer.[54]

The Alpha State

Look for a comfortable place to sit; do so, and close your eyes.

Inhale slowly and deeply.

While exhaling, visualize the number three in your mind's eye and repeat it mentally several times, saying: "three, three, three".

Then repeat this procedure with the number two and finally with the number one.

Be sure to visualize clearly; allow the number to appear brighter, or paint it mentally with colorful paint.

This should suffice for you to collect your thoughts and relax.

To attain deeper relaxation, you can transfer yourself in your imagination to a place representing the ideal spot for relaxation.

How long you remain in this alpha state and what you do is up to you. You can merely relax for a few minutes, or you can also enter your mental movie theater so as to have your performance transpire before your inner eye.

To leave this state, count slowly from one to three, saying that when you reach three you will open your eyes, be wide awake and refreshed, and feel better than before.

After a certain amount of practice, it will suffice to close your eyes, inhale deeply—and there you will be in the alpha state already.

To activate the process still more, we can utilize the "three-finger technique". It signals the message to our brain: "Careful!" and steers our attention in a particular direction.

Three Fingers

Lay your first three fingers together (thumb, first, and second fingers) and concentrate on what you want to do; for example, be composed.

Before you can introduce this technique as a trigger, however, you first have to program it.

Go into the alpha state, then, and say to yourself: "In order to attain what I want, I need to lay these three fingers together." (Now lay them together.) "This will bring me to that state of consciousness in which my ideas will be better registered."

Do this several times, and you will have programmed the three-finger technique into your inner computer, so to speak.

This technique is a valuable tool just before performances, and with it we can evoke certain desired conditions such as relaxation, composure, or security.

When, in the alpha state, we create a picture of ourselves in a desired condition, what is it we are doing? We are creating it, we are lending our ideas positive energy. When our brain waves slow down, our right brain hemisphere, the one responsible for creative energies, becomes activated. Here we visualize what we want to attain and set the switch for changes. With this kind of work, it is not a matter of some sort of mystical experience, but plain and simply a pledge for our life, here and now.

The following exercises with predetermined themes can be altered to suit our individual needs. I have selected a few useful possibilities deriving from my work with Assagioli's psychosynthesis.[56]

The Inner Dialogue

The technique of inner dialogue allows us to come into contact with our "inner therapist". In so doing, we can learn to count on our self instead of on the expectations of others or of other parts of our personality that only put us under pressure.

Relax with the method mentioned above to put your brain into the alpha state.

When you feel relaxed, visualize a summer morning. You are standing in a valley, the heavens are deep blue. Feel your feet on the ground, see yourself in your mind's eye, and take time to notice everything around you.

Your gaze focuses on a mountain rising but a short distance away. You decide to climb it.

You go into a wood; you perceive the odor of the pine needles and the dusky quality of the light.

You leave the wood and meet up with a steep path. Feel the exertion caused by ascending it, until you arrive at a large plateau at the top of the mountain.

Now there is perfect silence.

Some distance away, you see somebody—a wise and loving person ready to listen to you and to tell you what you want to hear.

Approach this other person, look at his face, his

smile, and the loving warmth he emanates. Pose questions or speak about your problem. You follow his answers, quiet and attentive. You allow the dialogue to go on as long as you like.

The discovery of our inner voices will furnish us with quite a clear picture of the pattern of our performance anxiety. If we can visualize these voices and discuss with them, we can gain distance—and our inner monsters and judges will take on an understandable form. In any case, through this procedure we will gain more freedom in dealing with them.

Reconciliation with My Monster

Relax and imagine a performance situation.

Find out which part of you is responsible for your anxiety.

Imagine how this part of you looks. Is it young or old? How is it dressed? What sort of an expression does it have on its face? Ask it what it is trying to achieve.

Is there something positive it can do for you? There is always some good it can do.

Ask it if it would be willing to continue to work for you, but in a way which could contribute to your benefit.

You can ask it to look out for new possibilities helping you to master new situations and challenges.

Have another look at this part of yourself. Does it now look more content, more relieved, older?

Thank it for having listened to you and for wanting to help you.

Reconnoitering Feelings of Performance Anxiety

This exercise will bring you into contact with feelings which contribute to your performance anxiety and will enable you to turn them into power in performing.

Enter the alpha state and imagine a situation of performance anxiety typical for you.

Employ your memory in order to summon up all the aspects of that situation in as much detail as possible.

Direct your attention to your feelings and bodily sensations. Imagine you were telling a good friend what you perceive.

If a particular feeling should come into the foreground, simply lay your hands on that part of your body and visualize healing energy flowing through your hands at that spot.

Hearken within yourself and ask your body if it has any answers for you.

Ask: What kind of feeling is this? From where do I know it? Did I have this feeling already as a child? Why does it bother me to such a degree?

Observe which answers, images, or ideas emerge from your unconscious, and your bodily reactions to them. Sometimes you will have to remain with a given feeling for some time, especially if it comes from an inner part of you to which you have not had contact for a long time. Your body will tell you when you should remain with a particular feeling or may pass on to another.

At first it might be difficult for you to interpret the delicate signals. With some practice, however, you will find out that your body is a dependable teacher. You will see that after this exercise you will feel more relaxed, both in body and mind. With time you will learn to develop trust and carefulness in your dealings with your own feelings.

My Performance

There is another way of dealing with guided phantasies, one less symbolic and more reality-oriented. Just as our inner monsters can unsettle us when they appear, our inner visions of catastrophic scenes can do the same. However, we do not have to be at their mercy. We can also bring them to a halt and transform them.

Some time before a performance, imagine the worst catastrophe that could possibly happen.

Check if your fear is truly justified, see how the phantasied catastrophe appears or what would result if it really were to happen.

Now paint a mental picture of yourself dealing successfully with the assumed catastrophe.

Visualize the composure and calmness with which you enter into the situation and cope with it.

How is your feeling afterwards, now that you have survived your imagined performance, on the next day, a week later...?

Another helpful version of this exercise is conjuring up a pleasant, positive concept.

Each time your catastrophic vision appears, imagine to yourself a pleasant performing scene—how you receive the applause, are embraced by friends, or afterwards are sitting over a glass of delicious wine.

Mental Rehearsal

A very simple visualization method is the mental rehearsal.

Before the performance, you imagine the course of events as realistically and in as much detail as possible. By this method, our body is prepared for the event, and our fear of the unknown dissipates.

Composure under the Spotlight

With this exercise, we direct our attention to a desirable inner quality: for example, composure.

Choose a quality that you assume will be helpful to you from now on in performing.

Phantasize to yourself that you already possess this quality to the greatest possible degree.

Allow this quality to take on as detailed form and shape in your imagination as possible.

Intensify it.

Now imagine that you are entering this picture and this form, becoming one with it.

Melt together with the quality of the picture and imagine how it is to possess this quality to the highest possible degree.

Feel how every fiber of your body is permeated with this quality, and how this quality embraces your feelings, thoughts, and intentions.

Finally, imagine yourself expressing this quality during performance, more than ever before. Visualize this situation as vividly and close to reality as possible.

Visualization exercises of a relaxing nature can cause pictures and memories of places and situations associated with rest, warmth, composure, and feelings of well-being to be summoned up. If we realize that we never cease to build up inner images, then it can become possible to learn to choose between different ones and to replace negative images with new, positive ones.

The Diamond

Such a positive alternative, for example, is the idea of the "diamond".

Go into the alpha state and imagine how a faceted diamond appears.

Regard the perfection of its form and allow yourself to be awed by its crystalline beauty.

Identify yourself with it, and feel how through it you come into touch with that part in you which is just as invincible and powerful—your self.

Anxieties, expectations, and the pressure to perform cannot affect this self in any way. It remains untouched by the demons of performance anxiety.

It is your core, the center of your being.

Realize that you are this self.

While the symbol of the diamond slowly wanes, allow your perception of the self within you to wax and to grow constantly clearer and stronger.

As we have seen, the basic principle of visualization—or guided imagination—is simple to realize. By no means is the effect of this creative work with our own power of imagination merely superficial. It stirs deep inner strata, those of our attitude towards life and to ourselves. Our inner ideas can either imprison us or free us. The choice is ours. Do we want to enslave ourselves to them? Or will we utilize their power to break out of the prison of our anxieties, so we can deploy new possibilities lying within our reach? In going for performance power, we should not allow the source of our inner phantasies to go unused. It is precisely by way of our inner ideas that we learn to recognize the various contradictory forces within ourselves. With the help of these inner ideas, we can learn to free ourselves from the control of those forces normally ruling us and develop within us the possibility of "nourishing" ourselves with positive experiences.

Like all tools, our imagination can be used in various ways, not only constructively. There is a danger that we try to avail ourselves of it in order to retire into a virtual world of wishful thinking, seeing ourselves consummating extraordinary or amazing acts without any relation whatsoever to our own personal reality. Our work with visualization will not be meaningful if we try to compensate for unsatisfied needs through daydreaming, but only if we produce ideas which lie within our reach. For this reason, exercises such as these can only be effective in the long run if we constantly try them out and transform them to suit our situation on a daily basis.

Affirmation

It is time to realize that we are not the victims of prophecies, but the prophets ourselves.

Closely bound up with visualization is another tool: affirmation. Already in olden times people availed themselves of this means. Think of the passage in the Bible: "What things soever ye desire, when ye pray, believe that ye receive them, and ye shall have them", and in another place in the gospel of St. Mark, it says: "All things are possible to him that believeth." Our thoughts create our reality. They are the driving force of our existence and a decisive factor in the mobilizing of our inner self-healing power. Depending on how we use them, we can influence our feelings and our body positively or negatively. Opinions can change; we can orient our lives anew if we guide our spirit in new directions - and this with the help of a method so simple that many people do not take it seriously until they have tried it out for themselves. It is understandable to doubt that a simple repetition of assertions and positive statements—affirmations—can be helpful. However, is it not so that we are constantly making affirmations which dictate our lives? Moreover, don't we tend constantly to make negative suggestions to ourselves? Such as: "Whenever I have to speak in front of people, I am always blocked"? Or: "If I only think of my impending concert (sermon, track meet, etc.), I get goose-pimples"? Think of TV commercials: don't they also work by means of affirmation when they repeat a certain assertion often enough that we finally buy that soap powder? Therefore, why shouldn't we, too, make use of precisely this powerful instrument? Why not change our old, restricting opinions and expand them beyond their former limits by the introduction of new, positive perceptions?

Affirmation work presupposes our firm intention to need or to wish for something in particular. Whatever your goal may be: if you can make a clear mental picture of what you want, and in such a way that it appears that you have already attained it, then you will be placing yourself in a condition helpful for the actual attainment of your desired goal. Your chosen goal, together with the affirmative assertion and the mental picture, require daily repetition over a certain period of time before they can anchor themselves in our thoughts. Affirmations can be thought, spoken, written down, or sung. They should always be phrased in a positive way. "I do not have performance anxiety any more", for example, is not good; "I am concentrated and composed" is a much better formulation. Since our unconscious mind takes everything literally, we should always remain in the present tense—not "I will become relaxed", but "I am perfectly relaxed".

"You can do it, because you believe that you can do it" (Virgil). In the final analysis, our belief is nothing else than a condition determining our behavior—a self-fulfilling prophecy. It is time to realize that we are not the victims of prophecies, but the prophets ourselves. We have the choice of fortifying ourselves with positive thinking, or of weakening ourselves by allowing our defects to appear insurmountable. The beliefs we have will determine how much of our potential we will be able to realize.

An essential factor in affirmation is repetition. This has to do with our unconscious, which is most receptive to repetition, because our energies are thereby channeled in a certain direction. This is a truth known to every religion and utilized in their rituals. If we work continuously with affirmations, we can change our projections: instead of living with fearful, negative projections, we can develop hopeful, confident, and optimistic ones. The use of positive projections onstage is an absolute must if we want to get our message across.

Affirmations have the power to influence us emotionally and physically. However, they can also be dangerous if we split off our feelings, trying to assure ourselves of being in a state that does not correspond with our reality. The affirmation, "I am totally in harmony with myself", will sound grotesque if it is uttered in a tone which tells us, "Don't you dare contradict me". Affirmations, therefore, can only be believable and effective if they are in harmony with our feelings. Just as with imagination, they will work if they are produced in such a way that they become a part of us and move us emotionally.

Affirmations

> Close your eyes and direct your attention to your breathing.
> Allow yourself a moment of quiet.
> Now think about a certain area of your life that you would like to change.
> Imagine how you would like to be.
> Feel this state.
> Make a pronouncement—simple, positive, and in the present tense—about this state.
> You can also choose a picture (a symbol) or a sensation, preferably both.
> Take your time, and repeat your pronouncement several times.
> End your affirmation, knowing that your intuition will see to it that the desired state sooner or later will come to be.

Affirmations and Feelings

> Choose an affirmation suitable for yourself, such as "I believe in myself", "I am performing my task", or "I am healthy and completely efficient".

Relax and repeat your affirmation several times.
What feelings come up?
Which bodily sensations?
Wander with your hand to that part of your body that requires your attention.
With each breath, send the words of your affirmation to that place.
Notice the changes in your body.
With your exhalations, release unpleasant tensions from your body; repeat your affirmation until you have the feeling that your body accepts it.

Dealing meditatively with affirmations and feelings seems valuable to me in dealing specifically with performance anxiety. If first we simply accept our negative feelings and then can let them go, we are creating room for new, positive beliefs.

Alert Relaxation

The relaxation reaction provides for inward-directed awakeness.

There is hardly an essay on the subject of performance anxiety that does not emphasize the role of relaxation. Relaxation is often taken as an exclusive means, because it is seen to be at the opposite pole to the "incorrect" choice of the flight-or-fight reaction and is therefore the "correct" reaction. The effects of the "relaxation reaction" are well-known: reduction of habitual muscle tension, better circulation, and diminution of stress and anxiety. There are countless means we use daily to activate our relaxation reaction when we turn our waking beta state "offline", such as in daydreaming, in performing a dull, repetitive task, or in certain rhythmic movements. Without doubt, stress reactions will be triggered less frequently when we practise methods of relaxation; but they are only *one* tool. They are not a substitute for our occupying ourselves with our "inner road map", which is essential.

However, readers who do not wish to take up any of my previous suggestions will still be able to obtain certain results if they faithfully practise any of the following proposed relaxation exercises. Five elements are necessary: peaceful surroundings, comfortable clothing, a comfortable posture, a mental tool, and the wish for relaxation.

Relaxation (1)

Sit comfortably, eyes closed.

Direct your attention to your breathing.

Imagine that with each exhalation you breathe tensions out of your body, rinsing them away like ocean waves.

Wander with your perceptions through your body, beginning with your feet and proceeding through your legs, pelvis, abdomen, chest, shoulders, neck, shoulders, and back.

Imagine that you become relaxed when you request every part of your body individually to relax.

Enjoy this deep relaxation and visualize a symbol (image, sound, feeling) representing this bodily relaxation. From now on, this relaxation symbol shall be your symbol whenever you may need it, one to which your body will always respond by relaxing.

Now picture in your mind's eye a place where you like to be. Transfer yourself mentally to that place, and drink in its atmosphere.

The flow of your thoughts is calming down. Your brain is turned off, it is relaxed and at the same time highly alert.

Now create a symbol representing this state of mental relaxation. Whenever you want to relax mentally, this symbol is at your disposal. You can call it up at any time.

When you are ready, think of the feelings arising from your interior, negative and positive.

Give yourself permission to transport these feelings to a secure place where they are well looked after. (For example, let your "Thou shalt" statements pass away like a cloud.)

Allow yourself the feeling of being safe and sheltered, and create your symbol for emotional relaxation.

When your body, mind, and feelings are all relaxed, you are in the alpha state, the state of your creative, regenerating consciousness.

The more often you practise this kind of relaxation, the quicker and more easily you will reach this state. Now count from one to three.

One—come back to your environment.
Two—affirm your feeling of well-being.
Three—open your eyes.

Relaxation (2)

I owe the following spontaneous relaxation exercise to Betty Scott, who has occupied herself for a long time with the subject of musicians' stage fright.[57] Easy to learn, it is a sensible possibility of an all-clear signal when fear-producing thoughts come up.

Sit down comfortably and relax. Close your eyes. Take a slow, deep breath through your nose, and hold your breath while counting mentally to four.

Now breathe out slowly through your mouth, push all your air out, and wait a moment. Repeat the entire procedure several times.

Count yourself down mentally from seven to one, at the same time saying to yourself, "deeper, deeper, down, down". Find some mental means of transportation that allows you to feel as if you are going deeper and down. Perhaps you might want to imagine you are descending into a deep lagoon. Perhaps you would like to take an escalator or an elevator, or ride a magic carpet. Whatever you create will be right for you.

As you mentally count from seven to one, visualize and feel yourself going down:

7 deeper, deeper   down, down
6 deeper, deeper   down, down
etc. to 1.

You can stay in this place of relaxation as long as you wish.

Whenever you wish to return to full waking consciousness, all you need to do is to count yourself up from one to five.

With each count, feel the blood going through your body and be aware of your heartbeat and your breathing. Notice how relaxed you are.

With each count, send good thoughts to your body and mind, such as: "My body is relaxed but energized", "I feel good all over", "My mind is clear and alert", etc.

On the count of five, say: "Eyes open, wide awake".

Whenever you want to work on a special problem, determine what it is you wish to concentrate on before relaxing. You can do this in the form of affirmations, such as "My blood pressure is normal", "My mind is clear", etc. Repeat your chosen affirmation several times while you begin with the slow breathing described above.

Our Inner Gossip—
Work on Our Inner Voices

By working with our inner voices, we will learn that instead of the old dominating answers, we can give ourselves new ones.

The goal that I am aiming for in my work with inner voices could be described as finding our own center, the place from where we negotiate with our inner voices and guide them, in order finally to harmonize their energies. Our work with our inner voices may well have a playful element, a touch of joy at experimenting. Why not? These voices not only deserve our respect, but also loving tolerance and sometimes even a twinkle of the eye, signaling: "Come on, now, we know each other". Now, how is it that we can become familiar with them?

We will gain direct access to them if we can bring to mind what kind of character traits or behavior patters inhibit us the most before performances. For example, let us assume that we are plagued by a judge who before every performance puts us into question, blocking us. Our work on this inner judge could begin by our willfully awakening the judge and giving him a form, shape, or color. In this way we create an inner symbol with which we can communicate. As soon as we succeed in visualizing the shape of this inner voice—it might be a monster, an animal, a person, or an object—we should give it time to manifest itself. Manifesting means: allow it to reveal itself on as many channels of our sensory perception as possible. Thus we can not only see, but also feel or hear what it is wishing to communicate. We come into contact with as many aspects of this entity as possible and give it an appropriate name.

Now we should let this entity speak and express itself. We will best succeed at this if we can greet it: "Well, judge, what do have to say to me?" Thus we approach this entity inwardly and establish communication; that is, we pose questions in order to find out what this part of us intends for us.

As soon as we have recognized an important inner voice, visualized it, and come into contact with it, we will have succeeded in establishing both a relationship to it and distance. No longer must we endure it and acquiesce to it; self-confidently, we can accept it and form it anew. Such forming can only succeed if we are willing to make peace with our inner monsters. If we are able to accept them as a part of us, one making an important contribution to our personality, they will lose their threat. We will then become able to grasp, understand, and influence them.

How does such reconciliation take place? The first step consists of entering into an inner dialogue with our monster. It would be best if we were first to concentrate on *just one* monster. Later we will be able to deal with the interaction of the various inner voices. Now we should ask our monster as to his intentions: "Why are you here? What can I learn from you?" We listen to him intently and allow him to get everything off his chest. We can speak to him loudly or softly, sitting or walking, our eyes open or shut. What is important is our readiness to listen to any possible positive intentions, hitherto unimagined, which our monster may have, to come to terms and to reconcile ourselves with them, and to accept them as hints for concrete changes we should make in our behavior or attitude. For this reason, we direct the next question to our monster as a giver of advice: "In your opinion, what should I change in my life?" We thereby make of our inner monster an ally, so to speak, through whose counsel we can negotiate about possible steps towards change until they become clearly recognizable as separate steps.

At this point I would like to suggest a possibility of dealing with our inner monsters, one related to appearances in public and thus aimed at gaining power in performing. After you have identified one of your monsters, visualize a performing situation. Go to your instrument, deliver that speech, climb up to the high board, practise your application interview: do whatever you need in order to simulate the actual situation.

Now make an entrance in the person of your monster, assume his posture, his tone of voice, his gestures. Appear the way your monster would, and exaggerate in so doing, so that an intensive scene transpires. Notice thereby how you feel, sound, and look. Collect your impressions; the best thing would be to write them down, asking yourself: Did I find this person likeable or not? Am I afraid of him? Which of this person's characteristics inhibit me when I am in the limelight? Which ones could be helpful to me?

It is worthwhile carrying out this exercise with all your various inner monsters. If you have written your observations down, it is informative to compare them to one another. You may even find out that many a trait possessed by your monsters could well be constructive for the activity you intend to perform. By means of this exercise, you should also come into contact with your inner allies. This way, you could learn what energies you have in common and which qualities your performance could then take on. The final question is as to how the energies of your monsters could cooperate with those of your allies, so that both parties could be optimally represented.

A client of mine who was to give a speech for a ladies' forum summarized her work with her inner voices in the following way: "It became clear to me that my 'timid soul' helps me to say no, because without him I tend practically automatically, unthinkingly, to say yes to everything... My 'mother' [another inner voice] could conceivably help him, so that he would only utter his 'no' in case of necessity; for example, in the ensuing discussion, during which I would have to defend myself."

Of course, it is not sufficient to know which monsters it is that are tormenting us. We must also learn to cope with them and to guide them. This means that we should develop the capability of choosing by ourselves, so that we don't fall back into this or that monster's trap. The better we study our inner monsters, the less fear-inspiring they will be. If we assimilate certain simple methods of inner dialogue, our capacity to give ourselves new answers instead of the old dominating ones will grow.

Our Inner Dialogue with the Voices of Our Performing Anxiety—Power and Integration

Now that you have got to know several of your subpersonalities and talked with them, you will be able to concentrate on utilizing your inner dialogue in a constructive way.

Make a picture of one of your subpersonalities in front of your mind's eye.

215

Notice every single detail (voice, gestures, movement, clothing) and look for a word describing the quality of this person.

Play with this word inwardly, pronounce it loudly and softly, sing it in various ways, and finally let a picture of it appear.

Speak with this new picture: What do you want from me? What do you need from me?

What occurs to you? Which picture appears in association with this word? If you were to give the picture a voice, what would it say? How does the picture feel?

Now let both pictures appear next to each other on the video screen of your imagination and have them move towards each other until they flow into each other, forming a new picture.

Give this new picture a name and ask yourself what meaning this word has for you in connection with your performing anxiety.

Draw your whole body into this word. Feel it and try to experience it to the full—in your facial expression, your posture, and your breathing.

When this state has come to its height, set an anchor for it: use the three-finger technique described above (p. 197) and, in a firm voice, say your word: for example, self-confidence. (You do not have to use three fingers for anchoring. Some other gesture, such as clenching your fist, will also do. I prefer the three fingers, though, because this gesture is unobtrusive.)

Be aware of the power of this word, and feel this power growing.

Repeat this procedure several times and feel how you experience it more strongly each time. This means that the connection in your nervous system between your

state and this word will be getting increasingly closer.
  Change your state. Form three fingers and say your
word, and notice how you feel.
  Do this frequently in the next few days, and you will
see that you can summon up this state deliberately as soon
as you form three fingers (clench your fist, or whatever
gesture you have chosen).

The idea of integration seems to me to be of fundamental importance in dealing with our inner voices. That is, during our inner dialogue we have to see to it that we allow each voice to have its say on an equal basis with the others. Sometimes this will mean that we have to silence a voice that constantly reiterates the same thing like a broken record or send another voice to the rear that is always getting into the foreground. Integration also means: to provide for a fair, balanced atmosphere.

Contact with Our Inner Place of Knowledge

Our unconscious has stored away our past, it knows our future, and it knows not only about us, but about other people as well. In our dreams we sometimes can gain insights, and if we understand them, they can offer us solutions and show us the way. C. G. Jung calls this unconscious knowledge "absolute knowledge". If our self-awareness weren't to veil this absolute knowledge, all of us could have access to it. However, there are possibilities of tapping this inner knowledge. We have to dim the blazing light of our self-awareness to open the gates of our unconscious. Here I would like to introduce two possibilities of getting familiar with those parts of our ego that can lead us in our search for performance power.

The Old Man / Woman

Close your eyes, breathe deeply a few times, and relax.

Now imagine the face of a wise old person, man or woman, whose eyes are resting on you benevolently.

If it is difficult for you to visualize such an apparition, you can also think of yourself as an old person.

Begin a dialogue with this person about your performance anxiety. Make use of his or her presence to pose questions concerning your anxiety and your performance. Perhaps this wise person also has something to say to you or has a present for you.

Dedicate sufficient time to this person, and say thank you and take your leave when you feel that there is nothing more to say.

Write down what you have experienced, add your thoughts and associations, and allow the insights you have gained to have their effect on you.

Three Gates

According to many old traditions, when we are in need of help we should turn to the source of our creative intuition. This is not a means available only to a few gifted geniuses or prophets. All of us vitally interested in integrating and harmonizing various aspects of our lives can use it. By creating a specific context in our imagination, we can more easily recognize messages that wish to rise from our unconscious; this is because they do not have to fight against the inner gossip of our thoughts. Such a context is offered by the illuminating exercise of the Three Gates. The basic concept of this exercise runs like this:

> Close your eyes and relax.
> Imagine that there are three gates before you, one behind the other.
> Now open them, one by one, taking your time to observe what you find behind each one of these gates, what you do, and what you feel.
> As soon as you have finished, write down what you have seen; amplify and evaluate the insights you have gained.

According to Schorr, the imagery of the three gates leads to the deeper levels of our unconscious.[58] I can confirm that this experiment very often leads to profound insights concerning one's own ego. Particularly those people who pursue creative activities seem to derive special profit from these sources of their knowledge, since they are receptive to them in general. However, it is not absolutely necessary to be an artist or a musician to dip into these inner springs. A certain openness for creative problem-solving and the courage to deviate for once from our brain's well-trodden paths will suffice to initiate new discoveries.

In introducing these methods in order to make discoveries about our performance anxiety, we should always be sure to determine what value they have for our public appearances. As opposed to the advice of counsellors or gurus, which we are not obliged to follow, these messages are of a very personal nature. They can perhaps be repressed, but not denied. We will find that the best way to test our inner insights is by making them concrete: that is, transformed into deeds. Integrating our inner messages into our daily life means learning to guide ourselves in a particular direction, one in keeping with the insights we have gained. Transforming insights into deeds does not have to be accompanied by dramatic transformations. Small steps will also suffice. Should change fail to appear, there is the danger that our inner insights burst like bubbles, leaving behind an unreal world in us. Small steps towards change can thus be startlingly unpretentious, but their effect is great. Here I am thinking of the example of a soprano who would eat huge quantities of sweets before every concert. Through work on her inner voices, she found out that what she really needed on her way to her concerts was a good walk; then, fully tanked up with oxygen, she was able successfully to resist every bakery.

To feel our performing power and to step confidently into the limelight, then, it is not enough to ground our bodies and to have our feet on the ground. We must also "ground" our inner work so that it will bear fruit. This also means that we should not try to do too much at once. Every insight must "click" into place and become stabilized. This takes time, and also periods of rest, so that our unconscious can continue to work on a given problem; for as we know, our unconscious also occupies itself with our problems when we are at rest.

Paradox Strategies

Performance anxiety is a part of us, one that we cannot simply do away with or change as fast as possible, but rather one that would like to change us.

Until now we have been occupied with guiding and influencing our performance power from the perspective of our body and from inside, by way of guided imagination, affirmation, and inner dialogue. Now we will deal with the reverse path: that is, how we can attain our performance power through outward actions.

First and foremost, "symptom prescription", postulated by Watzlawick, should be mentioned.[59] His point of departure is that we can deprive symptoms of their apparent spontaneity if we carry them out deliberately. That is, we prescribe ourselves to have performance anxiety. Instead of practising self-control and secrecy, we now make our problem public. For example, if we are to give a speech, we begin it by stating that we are highly nervous. This prescription of behavior contrasts mightily with all previous known attempts at solution.

As the reader will have correctly guessed, this instruction is directed towards the problem-causing, fearful avoidance of performance anxiety. The thought behind it is the following: we gain power over our problems not only by avoiding them, but also by being able to induce them. It goes without saying that it is not easy to carry these instructions through, for who wants to propagate his problem publicly? However, we should not overlook the fact that owning up to our weakness has the advantage of putting others in a benevolent mood, so that our self-fulfilling prophecy is led *ad absurdum*. This possibility also contains the interesting feature that even if we cannot bring ourselves to make our problem public, instead confiding ourselves to a friend or only thinking about doing so, we will experience a certain success anyway. Thus the simple fact that this instruction is going around in our head will influence our behavior to such an extent that it does not come to a repetition of our old game of pulling ourselves together and keeping everything secret.

The method of imagining the "worst possible catastrophe" is also an attempt at a paradox strategy. It allows us to creep up on our performance anxiety from behind, so to speak, when we visualize the worst possible consequences of such an affliction. In so doing, we should exaggerate deliberately. It is precisely by means of this exaggeration, thoroughly divorced from the bounds of reality and from what is possible or reasonable, that it is often easier for us to imagine more or less realistically what the real, possible, and probable consequences might be.

Another variant of the principle, *similia similibus curantur* ("Similar things are healed by similar things"), is described by Triplett.[60] He suggests that we select an aspect of our public appearance that worries us, concentrating on it in a relaxed state as follows:

In which situation is the worry likely to occur?

When it comes, what happens in the body? What thoughts and feelings bubble up with it?

The next step consists in a simulated performance. Relive the worry. Let the worst happen. Make all the mistakes you can: concentrate on having a memory lapse, stumble while taking your bow, perform as badly as possible.

Exaggerate every detail so that all aspects of the worry are clearly defined. Pay particular attention to the feeling that is provoked, and find out where it is located in your body.

Hearken inwards at that place, feel it, and inspect it with your mind's eye.

Relax now and take a few deep breaths.

Next, think about what your performance *could* be like without this worry. Consciously decide to shift the body into this new position—the way it would be if there were no worry.

Without the worry, would you perform with more

energy, more intimacy, more looseness, or what?

Whatever your answer, perform in that way now. Perform as you imagine you could if the worry were dissolved. Act as if it no longer existed.

After a pause—and perhaps after having alternated between the two positions a few times—ask yourself: What value did I find in the first position? In the second? What did I do to will the two different ways into being? How did changing my body affect my thoughts and feelings?

What measures can I take in the future to will myself to perform the way I choose?[61]

It will also be of value to perform this exercise in front of a friend or teacher, in order to strengthen the effect of willful summoning up two ways of behavior.

The above possibilities should show that we do not have to be at the mercy of performance anxiety, but that we have a conscious choice. We can choose attitudes, and this also means choosing alternatives more useful than our previous evasive games. Even if consciously evoking other patterns may perhaps seem utopian to us, it is a fact that everything that we are capable of imagining also belongs to our possibilities. For example, if we can imagine ourselves performing masterfully in front of a crowd, this means that this possibility exists within us, even though it may still be dormant. It is there, just waiting to be awakened and nourished. To be sure, we can also opt to do nothing, but then we will deprive ourselves of the possibility of giving ourselves, on our own, something we had thought comes only from other people: self-confidence.

"What would be so bad if...?" For me, this seems to be

the central question, aiming at the bullseye of performance anxiety, as it were. The answers I have heard always circle around the so-called "important issues", such as: "The others might notice that I am incapable". Even though the facets of the "important issues" are different for every person, in the final analysis the question as to the worst possible catastrophe boils down to the realization that *fear of performance is fear of life*. Behind the smaller fear challenging us "onstage", a greater one is hidden.

It is important to notice these feelings and thoughts impartially, without justifying or condemning them. Many of us are not accustomed to this way of thinking, since in our culture we have been brought up to judge and to evaluate. Besides, conscious perception can at first lead to a subjective worsening of our anxieties, one which often causes us to push them away. In reality, however, our feelings of catastrophe will change as soon as we cease trying to avoid them. Perls speaks in this connection of "taking responsibility" as a step into freedom.[62] Taking responsibility in this case means that we should acknowledge that our performance anxiety is a part of ourselves, not one which we can simply do away with or change as fast as possible, but rather one that would like to change us.

Drumming and Singing—
Possibilities Offered by Music Therapy

Novalis would say: "Performance anxiety is a musical problem."

As a music therapist, I witness nearly on a daily basis how familiarity with music can give us access to dimensions of emotional and aesthetic experience surpassing our habitual power of imagination.[63] We know that music can cause people to dance, sing, or cry, that it can awaken feelings of tenderness, love, and courage, influence bodily processes associated with pain reduction, and initiate healing processes. Here the issue is the way we can introduce music constructively and creatively in order to turn the energies of our performance anxiety into positive channels, transforming timidity into power. In so doing, we cultivate the insight that our body reacts to music with resonance, just like a violin string. Our nervous system is very much a "string" in this sense. We can strengthen or weaken its processes with the help of sounds and rhythms.

We will remember that performance anxiety can be influenced if we intensify our various symptoms. A "musical" possibility of doing this is drumming. We do this to discover the "music" of our performance anxiety hidden in us. Drumming with our hands on a drumhead—skin to skin— often provides us with more insights than our head does; for whoever by such playing allows his hands to declare what his performance anxiety wishes to express will attain increased self-knowledge. The feelings simmering within us which are often very diffuse, as well as the fear paralyzing us, will find an avenue of expression when they are vented to the outside. They thus become audible. By activating and reinforcing them, we make split-second decisions: how much beat do I need today to exorcise my demon of anxiety? Everything can be expressed without danger: our every perception, our inner chaos, our yearning for order. There is no right or wrong. There is only I, in the midst of my personal rhythm experience. This realization leads us to accept ourselves the way we are, free of fearful adjusting. When we surrender ourselves to our own rhythm, our energies begin to flow. We become thoroughly engrossed in the matter and not in brooding about it, and forces which have hitherto blocked body and soul become released. If we permit ourselves to give free rein to this arousal for a certain duration of time and not break it off too early, then a paradox becomes true: we become relaxed, because body and soul feel themselves to be one. It is assumed that this phenomenon is associated with the production of endorphines in the brain which occasion a pleasant feeling of well-being.

Drum rhythms are particularly suitable for working towards developing performance power, because they stimulate us to express ourselves strongly. They also render blockades and boundaries audible and reveal the power and energy available to us. Experiences of this kind strengthen our self-confidence, put our feet on the ground, and make us centered. When we have experience with rhythm, we are brought in contact with our own rhythms—breathing, heartbeat, body movement—with which we can meet halfway the overwhelming feelings performance anxiety often induces. Furthermore, drum rhythms most pleasurably give us stability, make us centered in a nonauthoritarian way, and create order.

Now that we have become acquainted with a possibility of intensification, let us deal with just the opposite: relaxation. There is a very simple method of relaxing just before going onstage: by humming or singing a melody to ourselves very softly. This is what mothers and fathers instinctively do when they want to calm their baby, or what children do when they feel themselves alone and unobserved, humming to themselves; and we can also put it to good use for ourselves when we want to calm our nervous system. We just hum a melody of our choice and become immersed in its soothing, pleasant sound. This activity allows us to collect ourselves. It slows our brain-wave activity and brings our two brain hemispheres into a harmonious balance. From playing tennis, we know that we should not hold our breath at the moment our racket meets the ball, for this makes both our breathing and our stroke falter. If tennis players hum a melody softly, they can automatically adapt their breathing rhythm to that of their strokes. As we can see, it is possible to use the technique of humming in many areas. Not only will it reduce our feelings of stress, it will also make us play better: both our power and our pleasure will be greater.

Use the gift of your voice, with which you can calm and relax yourself. Perhaps there is someone else who could hum a relaxing melody for you while you are sitting in a comfortable armchair and enjoying the sounds, so that you can attain a deep state of relaxation.

Precise Help for Specific Symptoms

Now that I have introduced various general methods, here I would like to deal with particular symptoms and with specific techniques that we can avail ourselves of while waiting in the "green room" just before a performance. (I don't know whether it is true or not, but this well-known designation for the waiting room of a concert hall is said to have been derived from the fact that musicians are often green with fright just before going onstage!) Since most of these techniques have already been described, I will mention them here only in a shortened form as a quick reference aid. In principle, in our work with specific symptoms we should first accentuate and intensify the symptom, and then release and neutralize it.

Symptom: butterflies in the belly

1. Shake and flap your entire body like an excited butterfly, starting with your head.
In so doing, let your tongue hang out.
See that the flapping gradually involves your entire body, allow yourself to make noises with your voice as well.
2. Hara Breathing, see p. 184.
3. Centering exercise: The Lake, see p. 185.

Symptom: cold, trembling hands

1. Exaggerate the trembling in your hands, continue it in your arms, etc., until your whole body is shaking like a leaf.
Go over to whirling, circular movements—like a windmill—with your arms extended over your head and back.
Increase their speed, and see that your arms circulate in various directions: parallel, opposed, left vs. right, etc.
2. Hand, Wrist, and Arm Relaxation, see p. 172.
3. A Quiet Place, see p. 174.

Symptom: moist, sweaty hands

1. Centering, see p. 184.
2. Speakers' Friend, see p. 179.
3. Imagination exercise: The Diamond, see p. 203.

Symptom: tensions in head, neck, and shoulders

1. Spinal Relaxation, see p. 170.
2. Muscular Relaxation, see p. 168.
3. Releasing, see p. 166.

Symptom: cold feet or cramps in the calves

1. Shake your feet and legs vigorously, take high steps, stamp, or do a flatfoot country dance.
2. Give yourself a foot massage or have one given to you.
3. Go into a squatting position and hold it; your feet should be parallel to each other and about 8 inches (20 cm) apart. Your heels are on the floor, and your body weight is resting on the balls of your feet.

Symptom: dry mouth

1. Loosen your tongue and shake it vigorously back and forth; wipe it with firm movements over the lower teeth, then the upper ones. Let your tongue flail around wildly and make sounds and noises at the same time.
2. Make your teeth chatter for awhile. At the same time, hold your forehead with one hand and your lower jaw with the other, and exchange hands several times. You will see that your saliva starts to flow freely. In addition, it is said that chattering teeth stimulate the brain.

Symptom: pounding heart

1. Becoming Calm and Composed, Becoming Still
Calmer, see pp. 166-167.
2. Composure under the Spotlight, see p. 202.

Symptom: confusion and lack of concentration

1. Studying Our Body, see p. 162.
2. Relaxation (2), see p. 209.
3. Breathing in Five Parts, see p. 179.

Symptom: negative emotions

1. Sit on a mat with your legs crossed, place your hands
on your knees, and close your eyes.
Relax the tensions in your forehead and around your
eyes, and concentrate on hearkening within.
2. Stomach massage: circular motions with both hands
simultaneously. Concentrate on the feeling of relaxation
emanating from from your stomach towards the outside.
3. Imagination exercise: Reconnoitering Feelings of
Performance Anxiety, see p. 200.

Symptom: listlessness or fatigue

1. Shaking exercise: imagine your body is covered with
a sticky substance that you wish to get rid of.
Shake your body vigorously and use your voice to
make accompanying sounds.

Enjoy your body's vibrations.
2. Cross your arms in front of your chest and hold your shoulders tightly with your arms.
Slowly bend your knees, as if you were going to sit on a low chair.
You will probably notice a feeling of warmth and/or trembling.
Remain in this position as long as possible, and then return gradually to your original upright position.
3. Drumming, see pp. 224.

Nutrition

Prevailing theories about proper nutrition are confusing and contradictory. What is touted in one book as the fountain of eternal health is condemned by the next one as practically lethal. Furthermore, these books are always saying: Do this! Do that! Of course, taken by itself, a particular diet may do just as little in eliminating performance anxiety as the most sophisticated relaxation strategies, since performance anxiety is primarily the result of insecurity with our own identity and is therefore a question of our self-concept and our feeling of self-worth. However, any discussion of performance power will be too short-winded if it is concentrated exclusively on mental or spiritual processes. When the biochemical processes in our body are in an uproar, even the best attitude will be worthless, simply because our body is not tuned correctly and is not functioning properly. Imagine filling the gas tank of your sports car with coca-cola instead of gasoline. Even though your car may look terrific and have lots of horsepower, it still won't run. In this chapter, then, we will discuss how certain foods can contribute to performance power and how we can counter stress with appropriate nutrition.

Much of what I am about to say may perhaps run counter to held opinions. For me and the people with whom I have worked till now, however, these ideas have proven themselves. It is finally up to my readers what they make out of these findings, for they will only be meaningful if we try them out ourselves and form our own opinion as to their benefit.

What I have said about bodily and spiritual relaxation processes also holds true for nutrition: it is not sufficient to recall at the last minute before a performance that it is necessary to eat healthy food or devour a certain product that furthers energy and endurance. Doing so may assuage our conscience, but our body cannot be tricked so easily. Furthermore, such a short-sighted act of will would condition our brain in a direction serving only to strengthen the alarm signal of "performance" with all its stressful consequences. A kind of Pavlovian reflex would be established, so that we would associate certain kinds of meals with stress situations. It is true that performance anxiety and stress cause the body to require increased amounts of vitamins, minerals, and trace elements; but we are not doing ourselves a favor if we create a state of emergency by means of an abrupt change in nourishment—that is, either by an exaggerated energy intake or renunciation thereof—only to fall back into old habits afterwards.

The view is generally held today that there is evidence for the presence of at least a rudimentary self-regulation in our eating habits. Expressed in another way: our body knows what it needs. This has been shown in experiments with babies as well as with persons in exceptional situations such as athletes, pregnant women, or sick persons, all of whom generally know quite well what they require. In my opinion, we should rely more on the wisdom of our body. We should hearken into ourselves and take our sensitivity towards certain foods seriously. Certain foodstuffs attract or repel us; we should cultivate such feelings. We will need time, contemplation, and awareness before being able to treat eating as a dialogue with our own body and soul. The process of eating derived from a state of leisure and inner collection is the ultimate prerequisite of trust in our own sensory perceptions. Whoever can trust in his own senses, thereby gaining access to his own state of being and needs, creates the most important precondition for being able to express himself in a sophisticated way and for establishing a public identity: that is, the power of discrimination. If we possess our own capability of discriminating, we will not require others as a sounding-board for the amplification of our personality, for we will have learned self-trust.

We can support the wisdom of our body by introducing our rational understanding, thus making clear to ourselves certain processes influencing our power in performance. There are foods which have a balancing, soothing effect on our nerves. Others stimulate them unduly and artificially. There are even certain kinds which do both—for example, sugar.

"Before every speech I eat a bar of Swiss chocolate." This admission is symbolic for many people who have learned early on that the taste of sweetness can stand for things pleasant or soothing, for everything that we love. And yet doubts are in order, for in the newspapers we can read about the less agreeable consequences. Too much sweetness can lead to an insufficient supply of sugar in the blood. The result of this is that our brain suffers a lack and goes out of control.

What happens to our body when we eat sweets before a performance? Shortly after we eat something sweet, our blood sugar level increases, only to return rather quickly to its normal value (approximately 80-120 mg per deciliter of blood). With certain people, however, it can happen after a meal rich in sugar that their blood sugar level drops into the realm of so-called hypoglycemia. The brain, whose cells require glucose—that is, sugar—for survival and appropriate functioning reacts particularly sensitively. A lack of sugar invariably leads to symptoms of deficiency strikingly similar to those of performance anxiety, even reinforcing them: trembling, increased perspiring, heightened arousal, and feelings of inner unrest. Thus with time excessive sugar consumption will lead to hypoglycemia and is therefore not the way to increase one's performance power.

What kind of nourishment, then, is conducive to the required composure? There is a trick we can pull on our organism: lots of carbohydrates in our diet cause the pancreas to release more insulin than usual. Insulin, which is a hormone, sees to it that all the various elements necessary for protein synthesis reach their target organs, such as muscle cells. Tryptophane, which is irreplaceable, reaches the brain, where by the mediation of insulin it is converted into serotonine. Serotonine is a neurotransmitter which can be derived only from the raw material tryptophane. If there is a dearth of the raw material, then there will necessarily be a lack of the transmitter. Our gray matter, piqued at such a situation, will react with ill humor, nervousness, and fear. Once the lack is removed, we are once again better tempered and can sleep better, and furthermore a state of composure typical of the British, one which they perhaps owe to their breakfasts rich in carbohydrates, will set in.

Which foods are best for a disturbed nervous system? The answer is clear and simple: eat lots of fruit and vegetables. Our body requires the least energy to digest fruit, and yet it derives more nutritional value from this kind of food than from any other. After a couple hours an apple is completely digested, whereas a piece of meat occupies the digestive organs for the better part of a day. If we look around in nature, we will see that many of the strongest animals such as gorillas, elephants, and rhinoceroses are herbivores.

Now, what about the argument that human beings require meat for their energy and endurance? I consider this to be a modern myth. Let us look at what our bodies require for energy production: first glucose from fruits and vegetables, then fats, starches, and carbohydrates, and finally protein. Too much protein produces an overabundance of nitrogen in the body, and this in turn causes a feeling of tiredness—just what we don't need if we want to be efficient! Not to mention the demands imposed on our kidneys by uric acid and on our intestines by the bacteria of decay.

I don't want to claim that the sole path to health is by doing without meat. However, there are sufficient arguments against meat, and my own experience tells me that we feel better adjusted and more peaceable after having decided to do without the flesh of other creatures. After all, there are those who have set us an example. Wouldn't it be flattering to be in the company of Albert Schweitzer, Mahatma Ghandi, Leonardo da Vinci, Thomas Edison, Socrates, Aristotle, or Plato, who all have in common the fact that they were vegetarians?

A last word concerning vitamins. Many of the well-known recipes against stress correctly emphasize the importance of vitamins of the B complex for strengthening the nervous system. Now, we certainly cannot maintain that performance power is weakened by a lack of one of the B vitamins. However, there is at least an indirect relationship between a lack of B vitamins and performance anxiety, for both have similar symptoms: nervousness, muscular tension, forgetfulness, arousal, and fear. Moreover, we now know that stress and anxiety tend to reduce the level of vitamins of the B complex in the blood. Therefore, a sufficient supply of this kind of vitamin is not only necessary for prevention, but it also alleviates certain symptoms of performance anxiety. Foods rich in vitamins of the B complex include grains, vegetables, and milk products; they tend to suppress the symptoms just described.

This book is not the place to go into more detail about nourishment. I will have to forgo explosive topics such as coffee consumption, fat, and oil. Here it is more a matter of sensitizing ourselves to the kind of nourishment that exerts a positive influence on our nervous system, so that energy will be available any time we need it. Imagine how you will feel when you provide your body with cleansing nourishment which contains a large amount of water and you already begin at table to care for your nerve tissue!

11

Never Again Performance Anxiety— Oh, Really?

I cannot guarantee you complete freedom from performance anxiety, nor is that the purpose of this book. However, perhaps you have now become somewhat more reconciled with your own performance anxiety feelings. Perhaps you also can make room for the question as to what would happen if their message were to require *you* to change in some way...

The attitude, "Out of my sight", makes performance anxiety into an enemy, because screening it out only estranges us from a trait which is only too human. Performance anxiety is an existential problem. In concentrated form on the stage set of life, it represents our fear of life, a quality which more or less deeply, more or less concealed, is part of the human condition. It is precisely through our anxiety that we are able to arrive at something like a higher level of our public activity, characterized not only by greater intensity, but also through our interest in our activity and in others. Showing ourselves in public allows immediate insight into our personality and our being. However, it is up to us what others are to make of such insight. Of course our fear is justified, for with every performance we find ourselves in a situation in which we have to prove ourselves, one in which we are required to hold our own in the presence of others. Failure triggers fear; and this fear is intensified and even incited by our system of society, which has made the polarity of "performance or failure" into the preeminent criterion of judgment on nearly every aspect of life. The one-sided principle of competition opens up a gap between people at a very early age, one into which seeps the poison of animosity and envy. Envy has many faces: rivalry and competition, pecking order and crowing, jealousy and penis envy, contests and wars. Without the component of envy, none of these would ever take place. Thus the fear within us, and all around us, of our strict inner judges is not unjustified. Strangely enough, it occurs in concentrated form in just those groups which by virtue of their common activity should stick together in comradely fashion: at colleges and universities, among actors and musicians.

Performance anxiety is not something we can use to show off with, all the less so in a society which has elevated making believe to one of its most popular pastimes. Nevertheless, I question whether that element hidden behind the scenes of our life in society—that is, our fear of life— should be seen only as disrupting, only as something negative. Is not a productive or creative element also manifested within it? Something which, if it were to be eliminated, would result in a human concern being silenced forever? If we were to eliminate performance anxiety altogether, we would also eliminate one of humanity's songs. It is not only its threatening aspect, however, which performing anxiety shows to us. Anybody who is active creatively—the athlete, musician, or public speaker— and has exposed himself to such feelings is also familiar with the pleasure of setting up new situations for himself, of risking a step into the unknown, and overcoming his own limitations. Performance anxiety from which we do not flee and which is not allowed to paralyze us, but which we face squarely and unflinchingly, can thus become a productive element for our self-understanding and self-development. It shows us where we stand in life and how much we have come to accept ourselves. It holds up the mirror to us.

I believe that the shyness of revealing ourselves represents an essential psychological force for our life in society. Sometimes called "holy", it directs us to an ultimate truth, something inviolable before which we bow our heads unquestioningly. The spirit of our times, however, is constantly propagating a blanket reduction of our barriers of shyness. This is seen as a means to self-liberation, and to such an extent that our rules of shame become perverted. Natural shyness suddenly counts for something shameful. Yet the reverse is true: shyness is even an essential quality, for it fences in the area of our inner life, where it permits creativity to blossom. It also protects us from excessive feelings of exposure and from intrusive curiosity. For all these reasons, shyness represents a fundamental defense strategy in areas of expression as well as perception. In the last analysis, shyness is a guardian of our inner truth. It always sounds an alarm just when we want to deviate from it, ignore it, or evade it. In practice, the question is whether shyness is thus a warning signal coming from the depths of our self, one to be taken seriously and summoning us to self-questioning, or if it is a neurotic signal indicating a deficient feeling of self-worth, our capability of accepting ourselves the way we are, or a tension between our ego and our ideal ego. If human beings were to lose their shyness, we would be deprived of an archaic instinct, one which animals certainly possess and which also guards them against danger. They would rather starve than prevail over their instinctive shyness.

To be shy means to keep our distance, to take pause, to show a holy hesitation. It is a buried treasure which should be sought but not raised to the light. In a word, it shouldn't be therapied away.

In this book I have demonstrated how we can find our performance power through a constructive use of the energy hidden in performance anxiety. This is a path leading to ourselves and allowing changes in direction. As a conclusion, and as the end product of our journey, I would now like to add one more element to this process, which I have described with the terms "let it come", "let it be", and "let it go". The decisive word is LET GO. We can only let go if we are prepared to admit that we have performance anxiety. This admission requires self-perception and self-confidence as prerequisites for allowing others to gain access to us. Said in another way: if I am to show myself to my audience, I must first be prepared to take a look at myself, to listen to myself. It is not a matter of getting the better of my anxiety with some kind of stratagem or trick. Instead, my fear must be able to come out of hiding and be allowed to develop fully, so that it can reveal its meaning. In facing up to these fear-producing experiences, we receive the chance of discovering and assimilating the hidden productivity—the power—within performance anxiety. Self-awareness, knowledge of the world, work on our body and our mind: these are the qualities demanded of us. Not changing character or facade onstage, but reconciling our private self with our public self: this is the challenge posed to us. Even though such a goal may sound utopian, we can at least try to approach it. Its criterion is not self-styling, but authenticity. Authenticity presupposes that we carry the compass of our being within ourselves. Authenticity has nothing to do with self-exposure, but rather with awareness of both our vulnerability and our value. What unites us as human beings? Neither our chameleon-like adaptability to the environment nor our supposed strength, but our vulnerability. Performance anxiety will only then be healing and lead to performance power if it does not change suddenly into that false utopia luring us with the promise of a world made only for beautiful, busy, efficient, and self-confident people.

A last word, one not particularly fashionable but all the more important: love. Our entire discussion can be turned around completely with love. Love and fear are incompatible. If we love and honor our listeners, we will lose all fear of them. Think about it.

Footnotes

1) Cf. Vladimir N. Iljine, "Kokreation - die leibliche Dimension des Schöpferischen - Aufzeichnungen aus gemeinsamen Gedankengängen" in H. Petzold and I. Orth (eds.), *Die neuen Kreativitätstherapien* (Paderborn 1990) (*Handbuch der Kunsttherapie*, II), 203-212.

2) K. Hartmann, *Zur Psychologie des Lampenfiebers* (unpub. diploma paper, Hochschule für Musik und Theater Hannover 1982).

3) E. Goffmann, *Wir alle spielen Theater. Die Selbstdarstellung im Alltag* (Munich and Zurich 1969), 221 ff. (original edition: *The Presentation of Self in Everyday Life*, New York 1959), 221 ff.

4) *Ibid.*, 19 ff.

5) B. Guggenberger, *Sein oder Design. Zur Dialektik der Abklärung* (Berlin 1987), 19 ff.

6) G. Böhme, *Anthropologie in pragmatischer Hinsicht. Darmstädter Vorlesungen* (Frankfurt am Main 1985).

7) C. Lasch, *Das Zeitalter des Narzißmus* (Munich 1982).

8) Goffmann, *loc. cit.*

9) T. Parsons, *The Social System* (Glencor, Ill. 1951).

10) Goffmann, *loc. cit.*

11) G. Simmel, "Zur Philosophie des Schauspielers", in *Logos* 9 (1921-22).

12) J. L. Moreno, *Das Stegreiftheater* (Potsdam 1924, ²1970). In German there are two words for "body", the narrower term *Körper* for our physical body, and the more all-embracing one *Leib* for both our physical body and what I would call our spiritual body. In this section, both Moreno and Petzold are referring to the *Leib*, which I have translated as "body and soul". (Translator's note.)

13) H. Petzold, "Die sozialpsychiatrische Rollentheorie J. L. Morenos und seiner Schule", in H. Petzold and U. Mathias (eds.), *Rollenentwicklung und Identität* (Paderborn 1982), 13-189.

14) H. Petzold, *op. cit.*, 159 ff.

15) R. Dahrendorf, *Homo Sociologicus* (Cologne 1958).
16) Z. T. Moreno and A. Barbour, "Rollenmüdigkeit", in Petzold & Mathias, *op. cit.*, 359-360.
17) I am referring here to the fundamental principles of Integrative Therapy. A comprehensive study of personality theory is to be found in H. Petzold, "Überlegungen und Konzepte zur Integrativen Therapie mit kreativen Medien und einer intermedialen Kunstpsychotherapie", in Petzold & Orth, *Die neuen Kreativitätstherapien* (Paderborn 1990) (*Handbuch der Kunsttherapie*, II), 585-637.
18) E. Husserl, *Logische Untersuchungen I. Prolegomena zur reinen Logik* (Tübingen 1980).
19) D. F. and A. D. Jonas, *Signale der Urzeit. Archaische Mechanismen in Medinzin und Psychologie* (Stuttgart 1977).
20) F. Alexander, *Psychosomatische Medizin* (Berlin 1951).
21) Jonas & Jonas, *op. cit.*, 30 ff.
22) L. Wurmser, *Die Maske der Scham* (Berlin *et al.* 1990) (original edition: *The Mask of Shame*, Baltimore and London 1981).
23) H. Petzold, *Mit alten Menschen arbeiten* (Paderborn 1985).
24) J. D. Wine, "Test Anxiety and the Direction of Attention", in *Psychological Bulletin* 76 (1971), 92-104.
25) B. Weiner, Perceiving the Causes of Success and Failure (Morristown 1971).
26) O. F. Kernberg, *Borderline-Störungen und pathologischer Narzißmus* (Frankfurt am Main 1979) (original edition: *Borderline Conditions and Pathological Narcissism*, New York 1975).
27) H. Kohut, *Narzißmus: Eine Theorie der psychoanalytischen Behandlung narzißtischer Persönlichkeitsstörungen* (Frankfurt am Main 1973) (original edition: *The Analysis of the Self*, New York 1971).
28) M. Jacoby, *Scham-Angst und Selbstwertgefühl. Ihre Bedeutung in der Psychotherapie* (Olten 1991), 77-78.
29) H. Petzold, "Integrative Dramatherapie und Szenentheorie - Überlegungen und Konzepte zur Verwendung dramatherapeutischer Methoden in der Integrativen Therapie", in Petzold & Orth, *op. cit.*, 858.
30) R. Triplett, *Stagefright. Letting It Work for You* (Chicago 1983), 31 ff.
31) A. Wagner *et al.*, *Bewußtseinskonflikte im Schulalltag.*

Denk-Knoten bei Lehrern und Schülern erkennen und lösen (Weinheim and Basel 1984).

32) H. Schmitz, *Leib und Gefühl* (Paderborn 1989), 45-46.

33) The article was in the German weekly newspaper *Die Zeit* from September 6, 1991.

34) Jacoby, *op. cit.*, and Wurmser, *op. cit.*

35) Triplett, *op. cit.*, and D. Pargman, *Stress and Motor Performance: Understanding and Coping* (Ithaca *et al.* 1986).

36) H.-E. Richter, *Leben statt Machen. Einwände gegen das Verzagen* (Hamburg 1987).

37) Cf. Triplett, *op. cit.*, 89 ff.

38) I owe this formulation to Christian Scharfetter (Zurich).

39) W. Harman and H. Rheingold, *Die Kunst kreativ zu sein* (Bergisch Gladbach 1991) (original edition: *Higher Creativity. Liberating the Unconscious for Breakthrough Insights*, New York 1984).

40) K. Graf Dürckheim, *Durchbruch zum Wesen* (Berne, Stuttgart, and Vienna 1954, ⁶1975), 11.

41) Pargman, *op. cit.*, 49.

42) Pargman, *op. cit.*, 49-51.

43) A. Triebel-Thome, *Feldenkrais. Bewegung - ein Weg zum Selbst. Einführung in die Methode* (Munich 1989).

44) From G. Park, *The Art of Changing. A New Approach to the Alexander Technique* (New York 1989), 258, but much expanded here.

45) G. Gauss, *Heile Seele - heiler Mensch* (Welersbach 1987).

46) P. Terry, *Mental zum Sieg* (Munich 1990) (original edition: *The Winning Mind*, Wellingborough, Northamptonshire 1989), 118-119.

47) From I. Middendorf, *Der erfahrbare Atem* (Paderborn 1985).

48) From D. Sarnoff, *Auftreten ohne Lampenfieber* (Frankfurt and New York 1990), 76-80.

49) From Terry, *op. cit.*, 120-121.

50) From Park, *op. cit.*, 258.

51) A. Lowen, *Lust. Der Weg zum kreativen Leben* (Munich 1979), 47-49 (original title: *Pleasure. A Creative Approach to Life*, New York 1970).

52) E. Coué, *Die Selbstbemeisterung durch bewußte Suggestion* (Berlin 1982).

Footnotes

53) W. A. Shaw, "The Distribution of Muscular Action - Potentials to Imagined Weight Lifting", in *Archives of Psychology* 247 (1940), 1-50.

54) J. Silva and B. Goldman, *Die Silva Methode. Das Praxisbuch* (Munich 1990) (original edition: *The Silva Mind Control Method of Mental Dynamics*, 1988), 18.

55) From Silva & Goldman, *op. cit.*, 19.

56) R. Assagioli, *Psychosynthesis* (Wellinborough 1965, ²1975).

57) B. Scott, "Relaxation Techniques for Better Performance" in *Journal of the International Trumpet Guild*, Vol. 8, No. 4 (May 1964), 17.

58) J. Shorr, "Discovery About the Mind's Ability to Organize and Find Meaning in Imagery", in J. Shorr *et al.* (eds.), *Imagery: Its Many Dimensions and Applications* (New York 1982).

59) T. Watzlawick, *Die Möglichkeit des Andersseins* (Stuttgart 1978), 77-80.

60) Triplett, *op. cit.*, 174-175.

61) Triplett, *op. cit.*, 175.

62) F. Perls, *The Gestalt Approach: Eyewitness to Therapy* (Palo Alto 1973).

63) I. Tarr-Krüger, *Verhungern im Überfluß* (Heidelberg 1989), 25-26.

Bibliography

F. Alexander, *Psychosomatische Medizin* (Berlin 1951)

R. Assaglioli, *Psychosynthesis* (Wellingborough 1965)

G. Böhme, *Anthropologie in pragmatischer Hinsicht. Darmstädter Vorlesungen* (Frankfurt am Main 1985)

R. Dahrendorf, *Homo Sociologicus* (Cologne 1958)

U. Füllgrabe, "Ursachen und Beseitigung von Lampenfieber", in *Neue Unterrichtspraxis* 5 (1974), 300-307

K. Graf Dürckheim, *Durchbruch zum Wesen* (Berne, Stuttgart, and Vienna 1954, ⁶1975)

G. Gauss, *Heile Seele - heiler Mensch* (Weilersbach 1987)

E. Goffmann, *Wir alle spielen Theater. Die Selbstdarstellung im Alltag* (Munich and Zurich 1969) (original edition: *The Presentation of Self in Everyday Life*, New York 1959)

B. Guggenberger, *Sein oder Design* (Berlin 1987)

W. Harman and H. Rheingold, *Die Kunst kreativ zu sein* (Bergisch Gladbach 1991) (original edition: *Higher Creativity. Liberating the Unconscious for Breakthrough Insights*, New York 1984)

K. Hartmann, *Zur Psychologie des Lampenfiebers* (unpub. diploma paper, Hochschule für Musik und Theater Hannover 1982)

E. Husserl, *Logische Untersuchungen I. Prolegomena zur reinen Logik* (Tübingen 1980)

M. Jacoby, *Scham-Angst und Selbstwertgefühl. Ihre Bedeutung in der Psychotherapie* (Olten 1991)

D. F. and A. D. Jonas, *Signale der Urzeit. Archaische Mechanismen in Medizin und Psychologie* (Stuttgart 1977)

O. F. Kernberg, *Borderline-Störungen und pathologischer Narzißmus* (Frankfurt 1979) (original edition: *Borderline Conditions and Pathological Narcissism*, New York 1975)

H. Kohut, *Narzißmus. Eine Theorie der psychoanalytischen Behandlung narzißtischer Persönlichkeitsstörungen* (Frankfurt am Main 1973) (original edition: *The Analysis of the Self*, New York 1971)

Bibliography

C. Lasch, *Das Zeitalter des Narzißmus* (Munich 1982)

A. Lorenzer, *Sprachzerstörung und Rekonstruktion* (Frankfurt am Main 1970)

A. Lowen, *Die Spiritualität des Körpers. Innere Harmonie durch Bioenergetik* (Munich 1991) (original edition: *Spirituality of the Body. Bioenergetics for Grace and Harmony*, New York 1990)

A. Lowen, *Lust. Der Weg zum kreativen Leben* (Munich 1979) (original edition: *Pleasure. A Creative Approach to Life*, New York 1970)

I. Middendorf, *Der erfahrbare Atem* (Paderborn 1985)

J. L. Moreno, *Das Stegreiftheater* (Potsdam 1924, ²1970)

Z. T. Moreno and A. Barbour, "Rollenmüdigkeit", in H. Petzold and U. Mathias (eds.), *Rollenentwicklung und Identität* (Paderborn 1982), 357-362 (original edition: "Role Fatigue", in *Group Psychotherapy, Psychodrama, and Sociometry* XXXIII (1980), 185-191)

D. Pargman, *Stress and Motor Performance. Understanding and Coping* (Ithaca *et al.* 1986)

G. Park, *The Art of Changing. A New Approach to the Alexander Technique* (New York 1989)

T. Parsons, *The Social System* (Glencor, Ill. 1951)

F. Perls, *The Gestalt Approach: Eyewitness to Therapy* (Palo Alto 1973)

H. Petzold, "Die sozialpsychiatrische Rollentheorie J. L. Morenos und seiner Schule", in H. Petzold and U. Mathias (eds.), *Rollenentwicklung und Identität* (Paderborn 1982), 13-189

H. Petzold, *Mit alten Menschen arbeiten* (Paderborn 1985)

H. Petzold, "Überlegungen und Konsequenzen zur Integrativen Therapie mit kreativen Medien und einer intermediären Kunstpsychotherapie", in H. Petzold and I. Orth (eds.), *Die neuen Kreativitätstherapien* (Paderborn 1990) (*Handbuch der Kunsttherapie*, II), 585-637

H. Petzold, "Integrative Dramatherapie uind Szenentherapie - Überlegungen und Konzepte zur Verwendung dramatherapeutischer Methoden in der Integrativen Therapie", in Petzold & Orth (eds.), *op. cit.*, 849-880.

H.-E. Richter, *Leben statt Machen. Einwände gegen das Verzagen* (Hamburg 1987)

E. Ristad, *A Soprano on Her Head. Right-side-up Reflections*

Performance Power

on *Life and Other Performances* (Moab, Utah 1982)

H. Schmitz, *Leib und Gefühl* (Paderborn 1989)

B. Scott, "Relaxation Techniques for Better Performance", in *Journal of the International Trumpet Guild*, Vol.8, No. 4 (May 1984), 16-18

W. A. Shaw, "The Distribution of Muscular Action-Potentials to Imagined Weight-Lifting", in *Archives of Psychology* 247 (1940), 1-50

J. Shorr, "Discovery about the Mind's Ability to Organize and Find Meaning in Imagery", in J. Shorr *et al.* (eds.), *Imagery: Its Many Dimensions and Applications* (New York 1982)

G. Simmel, "Zur Philosophie des Schauspielers", in *Logos* 9 (1921-22)

J. Silva and B. Goldman, *Die Silva Methode. Das Praxisbuch* (Munich 1990) (original edition: *The Silva Mind Control Method of Mental Dynamics*, 1988)

I. Tarr-Krüger, *Verhungern im Überfluß* (Heidelberg 1989)

P. Terry, *Mental zum Sieg. Ängste erkennen, Motivation steuern, sportliche Leistung steigern* (Munich, Vienna, and Zurich 1990) (original edition: *The Winning Mind - Fine Tune Your Mind for Superior Sports Performance*, Wellingborough, Northamptonshire 1989)

R. Triplett, *Stagefright. Letting It Work for You* (Chicago 1983)

A. Wagner *et al.*, *Bewußtseinskonflikte im Schulalltag. Denk-Knoten bei Lehrern und Schülern erkennen und lösen* (Weinheim and Basel 1984)

T. Watzlawick, *Lösungen. Zur Theorie und Praxis menschlichen Wandels* (Bern, Stuttgart, and Vienna 1974)

T. Watzlawick, *Die Möglichkeit des Andersseins* (Stuttgart 1978)

R. S. Weinberg, "The Relationship between Mental Preparation Strategies and Motor Performance: A Review and Critique", in *Research Quarterly* (1982), 33

B. Weiner, *Perceiving the Causes of Success and Failure* (Morristown 1971)

J. D. Wine, "Test Anxiety and the Direction of Attention", in *Psychological Bulletin* 76 (1971), 92-104

L. Wurmser, *Die Maske der Scham* (Berlin *et al.* 1990) (original edition: *The Mask of Shame*, Baltimore and London 1981)

Index